Policy Within and Across Developing Nations

Dedicated to the George Washingtons
of the developing regions of the world
Kwame Nkrumah and Nelson Mandela of Africa,
Sun Yat-Sen and Mahatma Gandhi of Asia,
Mikhail Gorbachev and Lech Walesea of East Europe,
Simon Bolivar and Emiliano Zapata of Latin America

Policy Within and Across Developing Nations

STUART S. NAGEL
University of Illinois

Routledge
Taylor & Francis Group
LONDON AND NEW YORK

First published 1998 by Ashgate Publishing

Reissued 2018 by Routledge
2 Park Square, Milton Park, Abingdon, Oxon, OX14 4RN
711 Third Avenue, New York, NY 10017, USA

Routledge is an imprint of the Taylor & Francis Group, an informa business

Copyright © Stuart S. Nagel 1998

All rights reserved. No part of this book may be reprinted or reproduced or utilised in any form or by any electronic, mechanical, or other means, now known or hereafter invented, including photocopying and recording, or in any information storage or retrieval system, without permission in writing from the publishers.

Notice:
Product or corporate names may be trademarks or registered trademarks, and are used only for identification and explanation without intent to infringe.

Publisher's Note
The publisher has gone to great lengths to ensure the quality of this reprint but points out that some imperfections in the original copies may be apparent.

Disclaimer
The publisher has made every effort to trace copyright holders and welcomes correspondence from those they have been unable to contact.

A Library of Congress record exists under LC control number: 97027228

Typeset by Manton Typesetters, 5-7 Eastfield Road, Louth, Lincolnshire, UK.

ISBN 13: 978-1-138-32709-2 (hbk)
ISBN 13: 978-1-138-32710-8 (pbk)
ISBN 13: 978-0-429-44946-8 (ebk)

Summary Table of Contents

Contents vii
Introduction xv

PART I POLICY WITHIN DEVELOPING NATIONS

1 Improving Developmental Policy 3
2 Win-Win Developmental Administration 9
3 Emergency Nations in 1996 17
4 Postwar Developments: Bosnia and Public Policy 29

PART II POLICY ACROSS DEVELOPING NATIONS

5 Peace Studies and Research Centers 43
   David W. Felder
6 Mini-symposium on Inter- and Intranational Dispute Resolution 49
7 Exporting Democratic Rights as a Product 83
8 Mini-symposium on International Prosperity 93
9 Global Policy Studies 111

PART III TEACHING DEVELOPMENTAL POLICY STUDIES

10 Policy Analysis Training for Developmental Administrators 119
    Vasant Moharir
11 USIA Win-Win Traveling Seminars 133
12 Proposed Policy Analysis Training Program 143

PART IV RELEVANT BIBLIOGRAPHIES

13 Developmental Policy Studies: The Relevant Literature   151
    Robert W. Hunt
14 Human Rights and Developing Countries   159
    Craig Webster and David Louis Cingranelli

Contents

List of Tables xi
List of Figures xii
List of Contributors xiii
Introduction xv

PART I POLICY WITHIN DEVELOPING NATIONS

1 **Improving Developmental Policy** 3
   Suggestions from Africa 3
   Supplementary Ideas Based on China in June 1989 6
   The Philippines in 1990 7
2 **Win–Win Developmental Administration** 9
   Ideology versus Technology 9
   Personnel Administration 11
   Financial Administration 13
3 **Emergency Nations in 1996** 17
   Meaning 17
   Social Indicators 27
   Trends 27
4 **Postwar Developments: Bosnia and Public Policy** 29
   Basic Concepts 29
      Bosnia 29
      Applicability Elsewhere 29
   Economic Policy 31
      Unemployment, Inflation and Growth 31
      Sectors of the Economy 32
   Social Policy 32
   Engineering and Science Policy 33
      Physical Planning 33
      Science Policy 34
   Political Policy 34
   International Relations 35

Legal Policy	35
Legal Issues	35
Civil Liberties	36
Some Possible Next Steps	37
Bosnia	37
Applicability Elsewhere	37

PART II POLICY ACROSS DEVELOPING NATIONS

5 Peace Studies and Research Centers	43
David W. Felder	
Educating for Planetary Consciousness	43
War and the Ability to Perceive Reality	44
Peace Studies Programs	46
Peace Research Centers	47
6 Mini-symposium on Inter- and Intranational Dispute Resolution	49
Disputes between Sovereign Nations	50
A Joint Perspective	50
Two Separate Perspectives	52
Disputes between Controlling Countries and Colonies or Quasi-colonies	56
The Alternatives	58
The Goals	59
Scoring the Relations	59
A super-optimum Solution	60
Disputes between Central Governments and Secessionist Provinces	63
Super-optimizing Applied to Russian Secession	63
Finding a Super-optimum Solution	65
Disputes between Conflicting Nations within a Country	67
Super-optimizing Applied to Civil War in Yugoslavia	67
Post-Civil War Dispute Resolution by Ivan Grdesic	69
Disputes between Conflicting Economic Classes with International Implications: Land Reform in the Philippines	72
The Traditional Inputs	72
The Super-optimum Alternative	74
The Pro-democracy Movement: The Uprising in Thailand	75
Causes	75
Remedies	76
Predictions	77
Implications from the Thailand Crisis Case Study	77

	Differences and Similarities between China and Thailand	80
	Examples of the World Moving Toward Greater Democracy	81
7	**Exporting Democratic Rights as a Product**	83
	Pro-US Arguments	83
	Exporting Democratic Rights Compared to Exporting Other US Products	85
	Case Studies of Bad Exporting	85
	Case Studies of Good Exporting	86
	Humanitarian versus National Interest Criteria in Making Foreign Policy Decisions	88
8	**Mini-symposium on International Prosperity**	93
	Exchange of Goods	93
	Improving International Competitiveness	93
	Evaluating Alternative Positions on Tariffs	96
	Getting Japan and Other Countries to Reduce Tariffs	96
	Negotiating Free Trade in Farm Products	97
	The North American Free Trade Agreement	98
	Exchange of People	99
	US Immigration Policy	99
	International Refugees	101
	Volunteerism in Technical Assistance	101
	Exchange of Factories	102
	Foreign Factories in the United States	102
	US Factories Going Abroad	104
	Exchange of Free Speech Ideas	105
	Trade and Human Rights	105
	International Copyright Piracy	107
	General Exchange Facilitators	108
	Dollar Exchange Rates	108
	International Economic Communities	108
9	**Global Policy Studies**	111
	What the Field Includes	111
	How the Field Differs from Related Fields	111
	Multiple Dimensions	112
	Current Developments	113
	International Economic Communities	114

PART III TEACHING DEVELOPMENTAL POLICY STUDIES

10	**Policy Analysis Training for Developmental Administrators**	119
	Vasant Moharir	
	Introduction	119

x Contents

	Philosophy behind Short-term Training Programs	120
	Scope of Short-term Courses in Public Policy	122
	Structure of the Course	123
	Size and Composition of the Training Group	124
	Duration of the Course	125
	Contents of the Course	125
	Methods of Teaching	127
	Staffing Short-term Courses	128
	Literature Used	128
	Contents of Some Short-term Training Courses in Public Policy for Senior Administrators	129
	Yehezkel Dror	129
	Philippines	129
	Hyderabad	130
11	**USIA Win–Win Traveling Seminars**	133
	Format, Implementation and Feedback	134
	Win–Win US Foreign Policy	135
	Past US Foreign Policy	137
	Win–Win Issues in South Asia	138
	Trade versus Aid	138
	Seceding	140
	Nuclear Arms	140
	Appendix I – PSO World Regions	141
12	**Proposed Policy Analysis Training Program**	143

PART IV RELEVANT BIBLIOGRAPHIES

13	**Developmental Policy Studies: The Relevant Literature**	151
	Robert W. Hunt	
	Restructuring Distressed Economies: Policy Reform and its Impacts	153
	Political Institutions as the Missing Component in Adjustment Programs: Perspectives on their Source and Impact	154
	Dialogues and Dialectics: New Synthesis in a Civil Society	156
14	**Human Rights and Developing Countries**	159
	Craig Webster and David Louis Cingranelli	
	Human Rights Data Sources	159
	Measurement of Human Rights	160
	Human Rights and Foreign Policy	161
	Explanations for Human Rights Practices	164

Index 167

List of Tables

2.1	Ideology versus technocracy in Chinese public administration	10
2.2	Super-optimum solutions applied to personnel recruitment	12
2.3	Elitism versus democratic sharing in rewarding performance	13
2.4	A super-optimum solution approach to tax sources	14
2.5	Dealing with the deficit	15
3.1	Data by country on people, food, politics, environment, facilities and health (CIA report on 1995)	18
3.2	Data by level of intensity, country, trends and people in need	26
6.1	Evaluating policies toward arms control	51
6.2	A super-optimizing perspective on US–USSR negotiations, 1990	53
6.3	The Philippine–US military bases	57
6.4	Secession of Chechnya from the RSFSR	64
6.5	International economic communities and super-optimum solutions	69
6.6	Land reform in developing countries	73
8.1	Exchange of goods	94
8.2	Exchange of people	100
8.3	Exchange of factories	103
8.4	Exchange of free speech ideas	106
8.5	General exchange facilitators	109
11.1	Win–win issues in South Asia	139

List of Figures

11.1 Win–win US foreign policy 136
11.2 US foreign policy for 200 years 138

List of Contributors

David W. Felder, Florida A&M University, 'Peace Studies and Research Centers'
Ivan Grdesic, University of Zagreb, 'Post-Civil War Dispute Resolution'
Robert W. Hunt, Illinois State University, 'Developmental Policy Studies: The Relevant Literature'
Vasant Moharir, Institute for Social Studies, The Hague, 'Policy Analysis Training for Developmental Administrators'
Craig Webster and David Louis Cingranelli, State University of New York at Binghamton, 'Human Rights and Developing Countries'

Introduction

Developing nations in this context refer to any nation that is seeking to improve its quality of life, which includes all nations. The emphasis, however, is on those nations that seem to be most in need of improvement, not necessarily those nations that are most rapidly developing. Nations in sub-Saharan Africa, for example, have recently decreased their per capita income, but they are still developing nations and especially so given their relative poverty. We will not refer to developed nations as if there are some fully developed nations that have little room for improvement. Instead we will talk about developing nations and relative *industrialized nations*.

The concept of *policy studies* refers to the collection of institutions that are designed to study the causes and especially the effects of alternative public policies. *Public policies* refer to governmental decisions that seek to improve the quality of life or at least lessen the severity of various social problems. Policy studies institutions include ways of handling relevant training, research, publishing, funding and associations. Public policies can be classified as economic, social, technological, political or legal, depending on what societal institutions or scholarly disciplines are especially involved. *Policy analysis* refers to the methodologies for determining relevant causal relations, generally for the purpose of evaluating alternative public policies in order to decide the best policies, combinations, allocations, or super-optimum solutions whereby all sides come out ahead of their best initial expectations.

As the title implies, this book is divided into 'Policy *within* Developing Nations and Policy *across* Developing Nations'. The 'within' material is concerned with improving economic, technology, social, and political policy. Those policy fields are directed toward providing widespread prosperity, useful innovation, merit treatment and democracy, respectively.

Political policy can be divided into three parts. The first is concerned with government structures, especially the relations between branches and levels of government. The second is concerned with choosing political leaders, which often involves a discussion of political parties, interest groups, public opinion and elections. The third part is concerned with administering government policy, especially problems of personnel and financial administration.

Developing nations are at a disadvantage in developing their economic, technology, political, and social systems because of a present lack of financial resources. Some are so lacking in resources, such as the Sahel countries, along the Sahara Desert, that they are classified as emergency nations in terms of lack of food, shelter, health care, transportation and education. Some have the additional disadvantage of being recently at war such as Bosnia, Rwanda and Afghanistan.

These developing countries represent a severe challenge to policy studies. That especially includes win-win policy analysis, whereby all major groups come out ahead of their best initial expectations. Developing nations may not have large expectations, but they have high needs. They cannot afford wasted resources, like rich industrial countries can.

The second part of the book deals with policy across or between countries. That especially includes the need for peace and for inter- and intranational dispute resolution. The disputes between sovereign nations have lessened, as have the disputes between controlling countries and colonies or quasi-colonies. Certain disputes, however, have recently increased regarding (1) central governments and secessionist provinces, (2) conflicting nations within a country, (3) conflicting economic classes with international implications and (4) pro-democracy movements.

There are close positive relations between peace, democracy, and prosperity. Partly for that reason, the United States has recently been promoting world-wide democracy. Doing so leads to peace and prosperity. That in turn leads to better customers, suppliers and investment outlets for the US and all countries.

International prosperity can be especially promoted by (1) the free flow of goods without tariffs, (2) the free flow of people without xenophobic restrictions and (3) the free flow of ideas including technology transfer. That kind of global exchange is being promoted by individual countries, bilateral and multilateral relations and by international organizations like UN agencies.

The third part of the book is concerned with training administrators and policymakers in traditional administration and in win-win capabilities. This training is being facilitated by such entities as the World Bank, USAID, the Ford Foundation, USIA, the European Community, the UN, international practitioner organizations, international scholarly organizations, and other non-governmental organizations.

The fourth part contains two extensive bibliographies. One is on developmental policy studies in general. The other emphasizes human rights. Such rights provides for free speech, merit treatment, and due process. Without such rights, even a country rich in resources cannot flourish or progress for long. As people become more educated in developing countries, they demand such rights. Doing so in the intermediate and long runs is likely to mean better policy and quality of life for all major groups.

Improving these long-run results is the main purpose of this book. This is a high but worthy goal. One might say 'How can we be oriented toward such difficult challenges and goals?' Still others might say, 'How can we not be'.

PART I
POLICY WITHIN DEVELOPING NATIONS

1 Improving Developmental Policy

The following 16 points represent public policy suggestions for improving aid to developing countries, mainly on the part of the United States, but also on the part of other developed countries. The suggestions were stimulated as a result of touring Kenya, Malawi, Zambia, Brazil, Panama, Okinawa and other places from 1985 to 1995. Especially helpful were conversations with leaders of the legal profession in various developing countries (such as the Malawi and Zambia Law Associations) and also leading public administrators (partly by way of the International Association for Schools and Institutes of Administration). Relevant places also include underdeveloped regions of developed countries such as the Delta region of the Mississippi, the Negev Desert in Israel and rural areas of western European countries.

Suggestions from Africa

1   More advice to developing countries is needed on how to make better use of *mass labor*. This is the main resource which most developing countries have. Perhaps studies could be made of the way China has used mass labor to build roads, schools and other projects with relatively little mechanical equipment and relying heavily on local raw materials. The projects created have much more value than the cost of workers' pay, although the workers receive a living wage. The surplus value can then be used as a form of savings for capital investment.
2   More use should be made of *soybeans* in developing countries to provide needed protein at relatively low cost in comparison to alternative sources. Soybeans can also be converted to a variety of desired synthetic food products such as hamburgers, although the conversion costs still need to be reduced.
3   Better use of American *corn-growing* techniques should be made with regard to hybrid seed corn, herbicides, pesticides and inexpensive fertilizers.

This includes plowing under the stalks after the harvest to provide good natural fertilizer, rather than burning the stalks or letting them decompose into the air.

4 The use of more *cooperative farming* would mean that equipment could be shared efficiently by way of machine tractor stations. The Soviet Union has been a pioneer in that regard, but the machine tractor stations could be used in developing countries by farmers who own or at least sell their crops, rather than by collectivized farmers. The stations, like American county agents, could dispense knowledge as well as equipment.

5 Low-cost, high leverage *medical care* would save the lives of children. High leverage means that a relatively few dollars can generate a lot of saved lives. This includes preventive medicine and measures for polio, infant dehydration, malaria, leprosy, yellow fever and nutritional diseases. Saving children greatly wins friends in foreign policy. Saving children, however, needs to be accompanied by birth control to have fewer children to save, and also by job opportunities for when the children become adults.

6 Better planning is necessary for the movement from *rural areas to urban areas*. Such movement is inevitable as rural areas need fewer farmers because of more efficient farming. Such movement could learn from the experience of relevant bodies in other countries, such as the US Rural Rehabilitation Service.

7 There is need for more *electrification*, including at least one electrical outlet per village. Perhaps ideas could be gained from the US Rural Electrification Administration.

8 Greater use of collectively used *satellite dishes* would increase access for television programs that originate in other countries. Some television can be highly educational, especially when books and other educational outlets are lacking.

9 More use should be made of *synthetic agricultural products* such as gasohol, ethanol and oil substitutes. Developing countries can learn from the experience of Brazil and of American corn farmers during the oil crisis of the 1970s. Synthetic fuels may cost most to make than oil on the world market, but developing countries need the foreign exchange for other things, and they have the raw agricultural materials for oil substitutes.

10 More help should be provided on techniques for crash programs to raise *literacy*, including literacy in English or other international languages. The successful experiences of other countries, including Cuba and Israel, in that regard can be helpful. Literacy and other education programs are high leverage in building human capital.

11 There should be greater use of *systematic public policy analysis* in choosing among alternative public policies. Here the developing countries can learn from methods taught at public policy schools like Harvard,

Princeton, Berkeley, Michigan, Minnesota, Texas and Pittsburgh. They can also benefit from the more practical textbooks used in such courses.

12 More emphasis should be placed on *increasing national income* in order to reduce poverty, and less on redistribution of existing income. If a country is 90 per cent poor and 10 per cent rich, spreading the wealth of the 10 per cent may result in the country being 100 per cent poor because spreading that wealth makes so little difference and decreases investment incentives. A developed country that is 10 per cent poor and 90 per cent rich can wipe out poverty by spreading some of the wealth to the poor, but even a developed country would be better off seeking to increase its national income so as to raise living standards for virtually everybody.

13 More emphasis on increasing the national income through a program of active *governmental incentives*, including subsidies and tax breaks, would be beneficial. This has worked well in Japan, South Korea, Taiwan, Hong Kong and Singapore. It combines the ideas of supply-side economics and industrial policy.

14 In seeking to win friends and influence, there should be more concentration on professors of *political science and law* in the universities of developing countries, since they train the future leaders of those countries, and also on reaching public administrators and lawyers, since they are among the present leaders in developing countries.

15 The United States and developed countries should be identified more closely with freedom of speech, fair procedure in criminal proceedings and equal treatment under the law. This should include active encouragement of these *basic human rights*, since they generate respect for the law and increased national productivity in developing countries.

16 There is a need for more *international coordination* by the United States and other developed countries in providing more systematic aid. This means coordination by way of such international associations as the United Nations, they specialized international organizations, the European Economic Community and various regional associations. The coordination should also involve more input from developing countries as to how the scarce resources of the developed countries might be put to better use.

These suggestions cut across all fields of human activity, but they have in common the role of political science, public policy, public administration and public law. This is in contrast to the more usual emphasis on economics and engineering. For further details, see such books as Edward Stockwell and Karen Laidlaw, *Third World Development: Problems and Prospects* (Nelson-Hall, 1981); John Lewis and Valeriana Kallab (eds), *Development Strategies Reconsidered* (Transaction Books, 1986); William and Arline McCord, *Paths to Progress: Bread and Freedom in Developing Societies*

(Norton, 1986); and Fred Lazin *et al.* (eds), *Developing Areas, Universities and Public Policy* (Macmillan, 1988).

Supplementary Ideas Based on China in June 1989

The 16 points mentioned above were generated from trips to Africa, Latin America and Asia prior to visiting China in May and June of 1989. The following points in particular were stimulated by that visit.

1 Developing countries have an even greater need for *systematic policy analysis* and governmental decision making than developed countries do. The United States government could make many mistakes over the next generation and still be a prosperous country. Developing countries, however, operate too close to the borderline of chaos, as regards their available resources, to be able to afford serious mistakes.
2 There is a need for *pragmatic experimentation*. All developing countries should not follow exactly the same model. They need to experiment in different parts of the country and different segments of the economy. That experimentation especially includes alternative ways of relating the government to the economy in terms of the marketplace, subsidies, tax breaks, regulation and anti-government ownership.
3 There is an especially strong need for putting resources into *educational development*. The introduction of new technologies is not so meaningful if the population does not have a sufficient educational level to be able to make good use of those technologies.
4 There is a need to encourage innovative ideas relevant to more effective, efficient and equitable development. This means encouraging a *pluralistic society* in terms of a free marketplace in ideas, especially academic freedom, freedom of the press, freedom of assembly, and multiple interest groups, as well as more than one political party.
5 *Competition* can be a useful stimulus, regardless of whether it is competition between government-owned enterprises, private enterprises or both. Competition can also be a productive stimulus in encouraging useful ideas in the academic world and elsewhere.
6 There is a need for setting *higher goals*, rather than being content with merely surviving or doing better than last year, so long as the goals are not totally unrealistic. Partly achieving high goals may result in greater accomplishment than completely achieving low goals.
7 There is a need for thinking more in terms of public policy solutions where *all* sides can come out ahead, rather than thinking in terms of tradeoffs

and conflicts between classes, ethnic groups, age groups, the sexes, education levels and other social divisions.

8   There is a need for more use of *positive incentives* like subsidies and tax breaks, but with strings attached. Those incentives should be designed to generate socially desired behavior and, especially, to increase national productivity. This can be contrasted to providing support for inefficient economic activities or support for those with powerful connections.

9   There is a need for more *professional training* in political science, public administration and public policy analysis, as contrasted to governmental decision making that is based on ideological considerations and personal connections.

10   There is a need for more participation by developing countries in international associations and other forms of *international interaction*, so as to stimulate learning from each other.

11   The United States needs to play a stronger role in the use of its subsidies, tax breaks and incentives to *encourage other countries* to adopt systems that are more pluralistic and less authoritarian and that are more pragmatic and less ideological.

12   Members of the Policy Studies Organization and others who have knowledge about policy evaluation methods should seek to share their ideas with scholars and government members from developing countries in *mutually beneficial interactions*.

For further details on some of the above ideas, see S. Nagel, *Higher Goals for America: Doing Better than the Best* (University Press of America, 1989). This book could just as easily have been called 'Higher Goals for China' or, more broadly, 'Higher Goals for Public Policy'; the specific and cross-cutting policy problems that it deals with are virtually universal. For a more global interaction perspective, see Marvin Soroos, *Beyond Sovereignty: The Challenge of Global Policy* (University of South Carolina Press, 1986) and S. Nagel and Marvin Soroos (eds), *Global Policy Studies* (Macmillan, 1990). The PSO-related symposium was presented in journal form in the July 1990 issue of the *International Political Science Review*.

The Philippines in 1990

The interactions in Africa and Latin America resulted in an emphasis on the need for various aspects of technological development. The experiences of the author in China resulted in an emphasis on the need for more appropriate political institutions. While in China, and especially in the Philippines afterwards, the emphasis partly shifted to a need to think more in terms of arriving at super-optimum solutions to public policy problems. Such solutions enable liberals, conservatives and other major viewpoints all to come ahead of their best initial expectations simultaneously.

This kind of analysis was applied in particular to five different policy problems in the Philippines: the minimum wage problem, commuting to and from Manila, reform, trilingualism in Philippine education and the American military bases. The minimum wage problem can be used as an illustrative example. Let us say that conservatives in the Philippines want to preserve the minimum wage at about 90 pesos a day, while liberals want it raised to 100 pesos a day. The compromise would be 95 pesos a day. The super-optimum solution might be for workers to receive 101 pesos a day, but for employers to have to pay only 89 pesos a day – the government pays the 12 pesos difference on behalf of all employers who hire workers who otherwise would be unemployed. In return for that wage supplement, the employer must agree to provide on-the-job training to upgrade the workers' skills so that they are worth more than 100 pesos a day. Each worker must also agree to take and pass the training program.

For further details on super-optimum policy analysis, see S. Nagel, 'Super Optimum Analysis and Philippine Policy Problems', *Philippine Journal of Public Administration* (1990), and S. Nagel, *Developing Nations and Super-Optimum Policy Analysis* (PSO–Nelson-Hall, 1991). That book is one of the first in a new Policy Studies Organization Series with Nelson-Hall, a publisher that is especially interested in policy analysis applied to developing nations, as are the acquisition editors for the PSO–Macmillan and the PSO–Greenwood Series.

Acknowledgements

Thanks for stimulating the writing of the above are due to Dennis Palumbo in his role as co-editor-in-chief of the *Policy Studies Review*. Thanks are also due to the USIA for funding the Africa trip, the Asia Foundation for the China trip and the Ford Foundation for the visit to the Philippines. Thanks are especially due to the many people in those places who provided information and insights and to the many PSO people who in the future are likely to be participating in the PSO activities that relate to developing nations.

2 Win–Win Developmental Administration

Public administration is the study of methods for improving and understanding how governmental programs are implemented, especially in terms of personnel, financing and accountability. This chapter systematically analyzes some recent developments in Chinese public administration. It uses a win–win or super-optimizing perspective, which emphasizes methods whereby all major sides and viewpoints in a dispute or dilemma can come out ahead of their best initial expectations.

Ideology versus Technology

The following points, which refer to Tables 2.1–2.5 clarify the letters, numbers and scoring of the tables:

1. Symbols in these tables include: C = Conservative, L = Liberal, N = Neutral, S = Super-Optimum, #1 = Group 1, and #2 = Group 2.
2. The 1–5 scores showing relations between alternatives and goals have the following meanings: 5 = the alternative is highly conducive to the goal, 4 = mildly conducive, 3 = neither conducive nor adverse, 2 = mildly adverse, 1 = highly adverse.
3. The 1–3 scores showing the relative weights or multipliers for each goal have the following meanings: 3 = this goal has relatively high importance to a certain ideological group, 2 = relatively middling importance, and 1 = relatively low but positive importance.
4. A single asterisk shows the winning alternative on this column before considering the super-optimum alternative. A double asterisk shows the alternative that simultaneously does better than the conservative alternative on the conservative totals, and better than the liberal alternative on the liberal totals.

Table 2.1 analyzes the problems of ideology versus technology in Chinese public administration. From the establishment of the People's Republic of China, in 1949, to about 1980, the emphasis was on ideology in evaluating alternative ways to implement government programs. That meant referring to Mao, Marx and Lenin, or to interpreters of them. The result, in personnel management, was to emphasize hiring on the basis of ideological loyalty and Communist Party enthusiasm, rather than technical skills. From about 1980, an increased emphasis was placed on knowledge of economics in administering a business program, engineering and physics in administering an energy program or other substantive fields for other programs.

Table 2.1 Ideology versus technocracy in Chinese public administration

Alternatives	Criteria	C Goal Equity $C=3\ L=1$	L Goal Efficiency & Effectiveness $C=1\ L=3$	N Total (neutral weights)	L Total (liberal weights)	C Total (conservative weights)
C	Alternative Ideology	4	2	12	10	14*
L	Alternative Technocratic	2	4	12	14*	10
N	Alternative Compromise	3	3	12	12	12
S	Alternative Both simultaneously	5	5	20	20**	20**

Notes:
1 Public administration especially refers to personnel management and public finance.
2 In the context of personnel management, ideology in the 1970s emphasized Communist Party loyalty. In the 1980s, technocracy emphasized technical skills in such fields as administrative science.
3 In the context of public finance, ideology in the 1970s emphasized heavy taxes on the rich and on profit-making activities. In the 1980s, technocracy meant modern automation in tax administration.
4 The SOS alternative for personnel management might emphasize loyalty to worthwhile communist ideals like equity and merit in the distribution of government jobs, rather than irrelevant party loyalty or mathematical skills.
5 The SOS alternative for public finance might emphasize taxation to stimulate entrepreneurial development for the benefit of the economy, rather than confiscatory taxes or mindless automation.

* = this is the highest total in the column before considering the SOS alternative.
** = this is the highest total in the column after considering the SOS alternative.

In terms of Table 2.1, the basic alternatives are ideology, technocracy or a compromise between the two. Equity was the stated key goal of those supporting the ideology alternative, this was, however, often only lip-service, since personal status was the real goal. Efficiency and effectiveness was the stated key goal of those supporting the technocracy alternative, but this, too, was often only lip-service goal: again, personal status was actually the goal of those with technocratic skills.

In the late 1980s, more emphasis began to be placed on public administration, as practiced in the United States, Western Europe and countries with American-trained professors and practitioners in public administration. This emphasis recognizes the importance of equity in government programs, including postal systems, elementary schools, urban transport and other government services that take a loss in providing services to the poor and many other people in order to provide better access and equity. That emphasis also recognizes the importance of efficiency and effectiveness, as manifested in the use of decision analysis, operations research, management science and other such generalist techniques to supplement the substantive expertise that goes with business administration, engineering, physics and other relevant substantive specialties.

Striving for equity and efficiency simultaneously is associated with the super-optimizing idea of enabling both ideologists and technocrats to come out ahead of their best initial expectations. With regard to personnel, an enlightened public administration approach talks in terms of opportunity to apply for and meet the entrance requirements in government positions. At the same time, high-quality standards, designed to promote efficiency and effectiveness, are set. The broadened perspective on public finance may emphasize income taxes to provide equity but sales taxes and other consumption taxes as an efficient way of collecting large sums of money.

Personnel Administration

This more general analysis is applied in Tables 2.2 and 2.3 to personnel administration and in Tables 2.4 and 2.5 to financial management. Table 2.2 looks at a classic personnel recruitment problem. Applicant A does well on the first goal but not so well on the second, although above a minimum threshold. Applicant B does well on the second goal but not so well on the first. The traditional recruitment approach might be to hire applicant C, who is a compromise in the sense of falling in the middle on both goals. The super-optimizing solution (SOS) alternative might be to hire applicant A in order to obtain the benefits of his or her high quality on goal 1 but to provide on-the-job training to improve performance on goal 2 to a level

12 *Policy Within and Across Developing Nations*

Table 2.2 Super-optimum solutions applied to personnel recruitment

Alternatives	Criteria	G1 Goal Decent wages G1 = 3, G2 = 1	G2 Goal (overpayment) G1 = 1, G2=3	N Total (neutral weights)	G1 Total X (G1 weights)	G2 Total Y (G2 weights)
G1 Alternative Applicant A		4	2	12	14*	10
G2 Alternative Applicant B		2	4	12	10	14*
N Alternative Applicant C		3	3	12	12	12
S Alternative Hire 'A' with OJT		5	4	18	19**	17**

Notes:
1 Applicant A does the best on Goal 1, but Applicant B does the best on Goal 2. There is thus a tradeoff that needs to be resolved.
2 The usual way of resolving such a tradeoff would be to decide which goal is more important. One would then hire the applicant who does better on that more important goal.
3 The SOS alternative might be to hire the applicant who does better on the characteristic that is harder to train for. That might be the less important goal. That applicant would then be given on-the-job training to improve the other goal. The result might be that the applicant hired becomes the better person on both goals.
4 Another SOS alternative might be to hire the applicant on the more important goal but provide training on the other goal. The result might be that the one hired improves enough on the other goal for his or her total score to exceed the performance of the applicant not hired, regardless of which goal is considered more important.
5 This is the essence of an SOS solution, namely to be the winning alternative regardless of whether one uses the goals and weights of any major groups, perspective or ideology.
 * = this is the highest total in the column before considering the SOS alternative.
 ** = this is the highest total in the column after considering the SOS alternative.

close to that of applicant B. Applicant B would be hired with on-the-job training if the nature of the skills were such that it is easier to train on goal 1 than on goal 2.

Table 2.3 deals with the conflict between the conservative or elitist desire to reward especially high performance and the liberal or democratic desire to have many people rewarded, even if lower goals are achieved. The SOS alternative might be to ask for even higher performance than the conservatives or elitists are advocating but to provide subsidized facilitators to enable more people to achieve those high performance levels. The subsidized facilitators might include skills upgrading and the introduction of new technologies.

Table 2.3 Elitism versus democratic sharing in rewarding performance

Alternatives	Criteria	C Goal Elitism	L Goal Democratic Sharing	N Total (neutral weights)	L Total (liberal weights)	C Total (conservative weights)
C Alternative	Reward high performance	4	2	12	14*	10
L Alternative	Winners of lower goals	2	4	12	10	14*
N Alternative	Reward moderate performance	3	3	12	12	12
S Alternative	Ask for higher performance but with subsidized facilitators	>3.5	>3.5	>14	>14**	>14**

Notes:
1 The issue here is how to reward performing well in public administration.
2 The conservative approach is mainly to reward those who do especially well, thereby creating a small elite at the top. The liberal approach is to broaden the definition of doing well so there are more winners of the rewards that are available.
3 If the conservative approach gives big rewards to the top 10% and the liberal approach gives small rewards to the top 50%, then the neutral approach might give moderate rewards to the top 30%.
4 The SOS approach might determine that the top 10% operates at a level of 8 on a 1–10 scale. The SOS approach might say that everyone who gets a score higher than 8 will be rewarded, but the SOS approach provides many facilitators to enable a high percentage to score better than an 8, maybe even higher than 50%.
5 Facilitators especially relate to subsidies to upgrade the skills of public administrators so they can perform better than an 8 on a 1–10 scale. Facilitators might also include introducing new technologies that enable public administrators to be even more productive, especially if they are trained with the new skills needed to use the new technologies.

* = this is the highest total in the column before considering the SOS alternative.
** = this is the highest total in the column after considering the SOS alternative.

Financial Administration

Table 2.4 provides an SOS approach to tax sources. The conservative alternative emphasizes sales taxes, which bear disproportionately on the poor. The liberal alternative emphasizes income taxes, which bear disproportion-

Table 2.4 A super-optimum solution approach to tax sources

Alternatives	Criteria	C Goal Stimulating investment	L Goal Ability to pay	N Total (neutral weights)	L Total (liberal weights)	C Total (conservative weights)
C Alternative	Sales tax	4	2	12	10	14*
L Alternative	Income tax	2	4	12	14*	10
N Alternative	Other or both	3	3	12	12	12
S Alternative	Decrease tax rates but increase total taxes with well-placed subsidies	>3.5	>3.5	>14	>14**	>14**

Notes:
1 Conservatives tend to emphasize taxes on consumption such as the sales tax or the value added tax. Liberals tend to emphasize taxes on income, especially progressive income taxes where the rates are higher on higher incomes.
2 The neutral position is to have both sales taxes and income taxes, but with the sales tax rates lower than conservatives advocate, and the income tax rates lower than liberals advocate.
3 Both conservatives and liberals recognize the need for some tax money to support the government activities they like. The super-optimum solution here is not to abolish all taxes: that would be undesirable to both conservative and liberals if it means abolishing the government activities they endorse. Likewise, the neutral position may result in a decrease in the government activities endorsed by conservatives and those endorsed by liberals.
4 The SOS alternative involves substantially decreasing both kinds of tax rates while at the same time increasing the total tax revenue by increasing the GNP tax base. That can be partly done by well-placed tax breaks and subsidies to encourage greater national productivity.
* = this is the highest total in the column before considering the SOS alternative.
** = this is the highest total in the column after considering the SOS alternative.

ately on the rich. A compromise is to enact both taxes but with neither kind of tax bringing in as much revenue as might be needed. The super-optimizing perspective seeks to increase both kinds of taxes above the minimum from the two alternatives in order to have sufficient funding for necessary government programs. They key element in a super-optimizing approach (as reflected in the policies of both Ronald Reagan and Bill Clinton) is to try to have a system of well-placed subsidies and incentives so that the national income and thus total taxes will increase, even if the tax rate if lowered.

Table 2.5 involves the important financial management problem of dealing with annual deficits and a large, and possibly increasing, national debt. The conservative alternative to dealing with a deficit tends to decrease domestic spending and increase consumption taxes. The liberal alternative tends to decrease defense spending and increase income taxes. The SOS alternative is an eclectic package. It seeks to increase spending, but spending designed to upgrade skills and introduce new technologies that will pay off in terms of a larger gross national product. It may use selective tax reductions with strings attached in order to reward productivity-increasing activities. This

Table 2.5 Dealing with the deficit

Alternatives	Criteria	C Goal Defense and investment	L Goal Domestic and consumption	N Total (neutral weights)	L Total (liberal weights)	C Total (conservative weights)
C	Alternative Less domestic spending More taxes on the poor	4	2	12	10	14*
L	Alternative Less defense spending More taxes on the rich	2	4	12	14*	10
N	Alternative Decrease both kinds of spending Increase both kinds of taxes	3	3	12	12	12
S	Alternative More Spending Fewer Taxes	5	5	20	20**	20**

Notes:
1 A fuller statement of the conservative goal might be (1) have a strong national defense, and (2) stimulate investment through low taxes on the relatively rich. A fuller statement of the liberal goal might be (1) have strong domestic policies like education and housing, and (2) stimulate consumption through low taxes on the relatively poor.
2 The SOS involves a reduction of taxes in the form of tax breaks designed to stimulate greater productivity. Likewise, the SOS involves an increase in spending in the form of well-placed subsidies designed to stimulate greater productivity. The increased productivity means an increased GNP, which means an increased base on which to apply the national tax rate. Thus the tax rate can drop and still bring an increased tax revenue and thereby have more money available for government spending, including defense, domestic policies, deficit reduction and more well-placed subsidies.
* = this is the highest total in the column before considering the SOS alternative.
** = this is the highest total in the column after considering the SOS alternative.

kind of perspective is especially associated with the public finance aspects of Japan and West Germany's industrial policy. It is also associated with newly industrializing countries of the Far East, including South Korea, Taiwan, Hong Kong, Thailand and South China.

This is a time of cataclysmic change in the People's Republic of China. Never before has the recognition of the values of public administration been keener. The country is now engaged in an effort to interact more widely with other countries. For this reason, it is incumbent upon the leadership to improve the competence and capability of the public service. Chinese scholars and observers of Asian public administration have described the underlying dilemma of an autocratic system of government coupled with the realization of the necessity for rapid change. Public administration is both a practice and a scholarly discipline. The primary emphasis of China is on improving the capacity of the public service. Scholars at the same time express a commitment to developing the field. The same is true of many other developing nations.

3 Emergency Nations in 1996

Meaning

Civil strife and government repression around the world are putting civilian populations at risk of death from starvation and disease. The 23 countries or areas identified in Table 3.1 either have humanitarian crises that are expected to persist or are recovering from earlier long-lasting crises.

Estimates of food and water needs are based on standards of 500 grams of food per person per day and 15 liters of water per person per day which includes all water needs. The standards were applied to populations at risk, both within and, in the use of refugees, outside the country. The needs of both populations can vary widely in actual emergencies, which include both natural disasters (such as earthquakes, droughts, floods, volcanoes, typhoons and hurricanes) and man-made crises (for example, external war, depression, inflation, ethnic genocide, civil war and revolution). A third category is emergencies triggered by natural forces, but worsened by bad societal planning (for example, famines, epidemics, forest fires and landslides).

Possible new emergency nations for 1997, in addition to the 23 nations included her, might include Sri Lanka, Nigeria, Cuba and Bangladesh. International responses include funding, food aid, humanitarian agencies and military force. Most important might be aid in developing more effective public policies.

The source of many of these data is CIA publications on humanitarian emergencies. This data gathering is part of the new post-1992 CIA concern for intelligence work that improves international trade, US competitiveness and the quality of life worldwide. The laudable and mutually beneficial higher goals are better US customers, better supplies, better investment outlets, better investors in US capital needs and better world citizens. It is ironic that, from about 1948 to 1992, the CIA and the KGB may jointly have been the leading cause of man-made death in the world by creating wars, death squads and genocide to keep socialists or communists out of or in power in Indonesia, Central America, Vietnam, the Middle East, Greece, Turkey, Chile and Argentina, among others. One should, however, give the

18 *Policy Within and Across Developing Nations*

Table 3.1 Data by country on people, food, politics, environment, facilities and health (CIA report on 1995)

Country	Persons at risk	Percentage of total population at risk	Potential monthly food (metric tons) and water (million liters) needs	Political environment	Physical environment
Afghanistan	4 million	19	60 000 1 800	Civil war intensifying Little government control Humanitarian situation one of the worst in the world Extensive landmines	Deserts; scrub-covered mountains Extreme temperatures Snow; summer dust storms; earthquakes; avalanches
Angola	2.5 million	25	37 500 1 125	Lusaka Peace Accord has stopped large-scale fighting Political settlement fragile Limited government ability to support relief operations Extensive landmines, banditry and skirmishing are continuing problems	Coastal lowlands Interior highlands Winter rain
Armenia	350 000	10	5 250 158	Country is reliant on undependable transport through Georgia Energy situation has improved with the start-up of Metsamor nuclear power plant, but the plant itself is a risk Landmines	Mountainous Little forest land Hot, dry climate Winter snow Earthquakes Droughts
Azerbaijan	950 000	12	14 250 428	Government's ability to provide humanitarian aid very limited Humanitarian situation dependent on progress of peace talks, economic reform, expanded oil exports Landmines	Large lowland Mountains in north, west Semi-arid Winter snow Droughts
Bosnia and Herzegovina	3.7 million	90	55 500 1 665	Humanitarian situation linked to outcome of Dayton Accords Major tasks ahead: repatriation and resettlement, reconstruction and landmine removal Extensive landmines	Forested mountains Extreme temperatures
Burundi	800 000	13	12 000 360	Becoming increasingly unstable Insurgency threatening government hold on country-side	Rugged terrain Deforestation Topsoil loss Silting of waterways
Cambodia	300 000	3	4 500 135	Humanitarian situation improving Political infighting, corruption and lack of qualified administrators hampering assistance efforts Extensive landmines	Flatlands Rolling hills Dense forest Low wetlands Earthquakes Monsoons Typhoons Flooding

Airfields	Ports	Rail	Highway	Inland waterway	Fuel		Medical
+	0	?	+	0	0	Infrastructure comment: health care system poor; non-existent in many areas; marginal facilities in Kabul; severe staff shortages	Physicians/1000 pop: 0.11 Hospital beds/1000 pop: 3.0 Immunization rate: DPT 33%; measles N/A Infant mortality rate: 153/1000 newborns
+	+	0	+	0	+	Infrastructure comment: heavily reliant on NGO/PVOs for health care and public health programs	Physicians/1000 pop: 0.07 Hospital beds/1000 pop: 1.20 Immunization rate: DPT 26%; measles 39% Infant mortality rate: 142/1000 newborns
+	?	+	+	0	+	Infrastructure comment: although severely affected by its war with Azerbaijan, support from expatriate Armenians (100% of vaccines and drugs donated) makes Armenia considerably better off than other Transcaucus republics	Physicians/1000 pop: 4.23 Hospital beds/1000 pop: 9.0 Immunization rate: DPT 88%; measles 92% Infant mortality rate: 26/1000 newborns
++	+	+	+	+	++	Infrastructure comment: suffered severely from its war with Armenia; internally displaced persons heavily dependent on NGO/PVOs for health care; health care system inadequate	Physicians/1000 pop: 3.93 Hospital beds/1000 pop: 10.2 Immunization rate: DPT 89%; measles 91% Infant mortality rate: 34/1000 newborns
+	0	0	0	0	+	Infrastructure comment: suffered from war damage; poorly equipped and staffed; power, water and heat unreliable	Physicians/1000 pop: N/A Hospital beds/1000 pop: N/A Immunization rate: DPT N/A; measles N/A Infant mortality rate: 12/1000 newborns
+	+	0	+	+	0	Infrastructure comment: supplies, equipment and personnel are in short supply; facilities are overcrowded	Physicians/1000 pop: 0.06 Hospital beds/1000 pop: 1.3 Immunization rate: DPT 83%; measles 75% Infant mortality rate: 112/1000 newborns
+	+	+	+	+	0	Infrastructure comment: some of the worst health indicators in Asia; national health policy initiated in 1993 with WHO assistance; poor maternal and child health services; shortages of all supplies	Physicians/1000 pop: 0.04 Hospital beds/1000 pop: 2.2 Immunization rate: DPT 38%; measles 38% Infant mortality rate: 110/1000 newborns

Table 3.1 continued

Country	Persons at risk	Percentage of total population at risk	Potential monthly food (metric tons) and water (million liters) needs	Political environment	Physical environment
Croatia	500 000	10	7 500	Humanitarian situation dependent on peaceful reintegration of Eastern Slavonia	Interior plains: hot summer; winter snow
			255	Extensive landmines	Coastal highlands: dry summer, mild winter
Eritrea	1 million	28	15 000	Postwar recovery continuing Postwar security problems continue Faces long-term feeding	Loss of infrastructure due to war Highlands extend in a north–south direction
			450	problem due to risk of drought Extensive landmines	Hot desert east coastal plain Northwest hilly/southwest plains Cooler and wetter west hills and plains Droughts
Ethiopia	3–4 million	5–7	45 000– 60 000	Postwar recovery continuing Ethnic tensions appear manageable Security tenuous in parts of countryside	Infrastructure unable to support large-scale relief operations Crop failures Drought
			1 350– 1 800	Faces long-term feeding problem due to risk of drought Extensive landmines	Extreme temperatures Intense sunlight
Georgia	1 million	17	15 000	Government dependent on west for humanitarian and other aid Humanitarian improvement depends on continuation of	Mountains: cold, snowy winters Lowlands near Black Sea: mild winter, dry summer
			450	ceasefires, economic reforms and continued international support Landmines	
Haiti	900 000– 1.3 million	14–20	13 500– 19 000	Economic recovery is slow; unemployment rate at 70 per cent Security still a problem despite new police force	Mountains Summer rains Warm humid year round Hurricanes
			405–585		Earthquakes Infrastructure is poor and unreliable Soil depleted Watershed damage
Iraq	>1.3–<4.0 million	6–19	19 500– 60 000	Difficult humanitarian situation linked to government refusal to accept UN conditions Government-subsidized food rations have been cut in central and southern Iraq	Mostly flat Northern mountains Desert Freezing temperatures in north and desert
			585– 1 800	Relief operation has improved living conditions in the north Extensive landmines	Dust/sandstorms Heat/dehydration

Emergency Nations in 1996 21

Airfields	Ports	Rail	Highway	Inland waterway	Fuel	Infrastructure comment	Medical
+	++	+	++	+	++	Infrastructure comment: tertiary care facilities in major cities relatively good: adequate equipment/staffing; occasional medical supply shortages	Physicians/1000 pop: N/A Hospital beds/1000 pop: N/A Immunization rate: DPT N/A; measles N/A Infant mortality rate: 8/1000 newborns
0	+	0	+	?	0	Infrastructure comment: Eritrean health care system is undergoing a slow transition from a highly mobile military-based system to a nationwide, civilian one	Physicians/1000 pop: 0.02 Hospital beds/1000 pop: 0.5 Immunization rate: DPT N/A; measles N/A Infant mortality rate: 121/1000 newborns
0	?	0	+	0	0	Infrastructure comment: Ethiopian medical system depends heavily on numerous NGOs and foreign medical assistance programs	Physicians/1000 pop: 0.03 Hospital beds/1000 pop: 0.3 Immunization rate: DPT 44%; measles 37% Infant mortality rate: 121/1000 newborns
+	++	+	+	+	+	Infrastructure comment: civil war and ethnic conflict have resulted in economic ruin, contributing to almost total collapse of health care infrastructure	Physicians/1000 pop: 5.92 Hospital beds/1000 pop: 11.10 Immunization rate: DPT 65%; measles 74% Infant mortality rate: 23/1000 newborns
+	+	0	0	?	0	Infrastructure comment: medical infrastructure probably will improve as a result of the influx of foreign assistance following President Aristide's return to power	Physicians/1000 pop: .22 Hospital beds/1000 pop: .77 Immunization rate: DPT 41%; measles 31% Infant mortality rate: 101/1000 newborns
++	+	+	++	0	++	Infrastructure comment: Iraq's health care sector can provide only rudimentary care; a war or natural disaster would quickly overwhelm the entire health care system	Physicians/1000 pop: 0.58 Hospital beds/1000 pop: 1.6 Immunization rate: DPT 69%; measles 73% Infant mortality rate: 62/1000 newborns

Table 3.1 continued

Country	Persons at risk	Percentage of total population at risk	Potential monthly food (metric tons) and water (million liters) needs	Political environment	Physical environment
Liberia	1.5 million	49	22 500 675	August 1995 ceasefire holding Scattered skirmishes among warring factions continuing Country's physical and economic infrastructure largely destroyed Landmines	Flat Little forest land Hot and humid Rainy and dry seasons
Mozambique	400 000	2	6 000 180	Fragile peace holding Banditry a problem Economy and infrastructure devastated Drought and poor harvests occurred in the southern provinces in 1995 Extensive landmines	Plains Forested plateaus Subtropical south Tropical center and north October–November rains
North Korea	N/A	N/A	N/A	Grain harvest short of country's needs Press and international relief agency reporting indicates serious food shortages	Mostly rugged hill and mountains Coastal plains wide in west/discontinuous in east Temperate climate with rainfall concentrated in summer Winters dry and cold Typhoons Floods
Russia (Chechnya)	300 000	27	4 500 135	Groznyy's infrastructure being restored Elsewhere repairs lagging; agriculture hampered Landmines	South: harsh, snowy winters; mild summers Northern semi-arid plains: mild winters; warm summers South/central river valleys: dense winter fog Extensive damage to infrastructure
Rwanda	2.5 million	29	37 000 1 125	Humanitarian situation has stabilized Refugees reluctant to return voluntarily Extensive landmines	Highlands Scattered plains Tropical climate Regional differences Winter rains Short, dry summer
Sierra Leone	1.8 million	38	27 000 810	Collapsed state No end of civil war in sight Extensive landmines	Swamps; beaches Low plains Highlands Tropical climate Constant heat and humidity

Airfields	Ports	Rail	Highway	Inland waterway	Fuel		Medical
+	+	0	+	0	0	Infrastructure comment: 36 hospitals existed before current conflict; all are now damaged or destroyed; personnel poorly trained	Physicians/1000 pop: N/A Hospital beds/1000 pop: N/A Immunization rate: DPT N/A; measles N/A Infant mortality rate: 111/1000 newborns
+	+	+	+	0	0	Infrastructure comment: emerging from the civil war, Mozambique is rebuilding; the government receives health care assistance from many countries and relief agencies	Physicians/1000 pop: 0.02 Hospital beds/1000 pop: 0.90 Immunization rate: DPT 19%; measles 23% Infant mortality rate: 126/1000 newborns
++	++	++	++	++	+	Infrastructure comment: North Korea's isolation is reflected in its health care system, which can provide only rudimentary care to segments of its population; war/natural disaster could quickly overwhelm the system	Physicians/1000 pop: 2.72 Hospital beds/1000 pop: 13.50 Immunization rate: DPT 45%; measles 48% Infant mortality rate: 27/1000 newborns
++	+	++	+	+	?	Infrastructure comment: clinical services and public health infrastructure in Chechnya, and especially Grozny, almost completely destroyed by ongoing war; the void in services partially filled by NGO/PVOs	Physicians/1000 pop: 4.69 Hospital beds/1000 pop: 13.8 Immunization rate: DPT N/A; measles N/A Infant mortality rate: N/A
+	+	0	+	+	0	Infrastructure comment: the ongoing conflict and refugee situation have had a serious impact on the country's health care system	Physicians/1000 pop: 0.02 Hospital beds/1000 pop: 1.70 Immunization rate: DPT 89%; measles 89% Infant mortality rate: 118/1000 newborns
+	+	0	+	0	0	Infrastructure comments: some qualified physicians; facilities and equipment poor; shortages of supplies; substandard care	Physicians/1000 pop: 0.07 Hospital beds/1000 pop: 1.0 Immunization rate: DPT 75%; measles 74% Infant mortality rate: 139/1000 newborns

Table 3.1 continued

Country	Persons at risk	Percentage of total population at risk	Potential monthly food (metric tons) and water (million liters) needs	Political environment	Physical environment
Somalia	1 million	14	15 000 450	No central government authority exists Clan skirmishes disrupting relief assistance and planting of crops Landmines	Large plateau Coastal plain Mountains in north Sparse rain Severe heat Drought
Sri Lanka	850 000	5	12 750 383	Civil war intensifying in north and east Government restricting NGO aid deliveries Extensive landmines	Infrastructure marginally capable of supporting relief operations Deforestation Soil depletion Water scarcity High temperatures and humidity
Sudan	4 million	13	60 000 1 800	Civil war has intensified All sides use relief as weapon Government opposes relief to south and to non-Muslims in north Extensive landmines	Desert, extreme heat in north Swamp, forest, flooding in south Infrastructure unable to support relief operations
Tajikistan	1 million	16	15 000 450	Government has consolidated control over most of country Dependent on international assistance to meet population's basic needs Landmines	Mountainous Semi-arid lower areas

Notes:
1. Transport infrastructure: ++ = supports relief effort; + = supports limited effort; 0 = support nil or severely constrained.
2. Fuel infrastructure: ++ = extensive; + = limited; 0 = very limited.

Emergency Nations in 1996   25

Airfields	Ports	Rail	Highway	Inland waterway	Fuel		Medical
++	++	0	+	0	0	Infrastructure comment: the civil war severely disrupted the country's medical infrastructure and capabilities; Somalia has no functioning government; foreign assistance still required	Physicians/1000 pop: 0.07 Hospital beds/1000 pop: 0.80 Immunization rate: DPT 18%; measles 30% Infant mortality rate: 120/1000 newborns
+	+	0	+	0	+	Infrastructure comment: Columbo facilities approach western quality; health care in north and east disrupted by fighting	Physicians/1000 pop: 0.14 Hospital beds/1000 pop: 2.8 Immunization rate: DPT 86%; measles 79% Infant mortality rate: 21/1000 newborns
+	+	+	+	+	+	Infrastructure comment: 164 hospitals are old, crowded and unsanitary; large outflow of doctors with formation of Eritrea; critical shortages of personnel and supplies	Physicians/1000 pop: 0.09 Hospital beds/1000 pop: 0.90 Immunization rate: DPT 63%; measles 58% Infant mortality rate: 78/1000 newborns
+	0	+	+	0	0	Infrastructure comment: system heavily dependent on humanitarian assistance and is in poor condition; continuing tribal and ethnic conflicts complicate health care delivery and access	Physicians/1000 pop: 2.71 Hospital beds/1000 pop: 10.60 Immunization rate: DPT 89%; measles 89% Infant mortality rate: 60/1000 newborns

26 *Policy Within and Across Developing Nations*

Table 3.2 Data by level of intensity, country, trends and people in need

Situation (levels)	Country	Humanitarian situation in the country during 1995	People in need (millions)	
			Dec. 94	Dec. 95
Intense conflicts (Level 1)	Afghanistan	worsened	4.2	4.0
	Burundi	worsened	0.9	0.8
	Sierra Leone	worsened	1.1	1.8
Simmering conflicts (Level 2)	Russia (Chechnya)	worsened, then leveled off	N/A	0.3
	Rwanda	improved	4.0	2.5
	Somalia	worsened	1.1	1.0
	Sri Lanka	worsened	0.7	0.85
	Sudan	improved, then worsened	4.3	4.0
	Tajikistan	improved	1.0	1.0
Government repression in rogue states (Level 3)	Iraq:		1.3	>1.3–<4.0
	Central/southern	worsened		
	Kurdish north	improved		
	North Korea	worsened	Unknown	
Ceasefires cessation of hostilities (Level 4)	Armenia	leveled off	0.3	0.35
	Azerbaijan	leveled off	1.0	0.95
	Georgia	leveled off	1.0	1.0
Political settlements being implemented (Level 5)	Angola	improved	3.7	2.5
	Bosnia and Herzegovina	worsened, then improved	3.8	3.7
	Croatia	worsened, then improved	0.5	0.5
	Haiti	leveled off	1.3	0.9–1.3
	Liberia	worsened, then improved	2.1	1.5
Post-crises mop-up (Level 6)	Cambodia	improved	0.3	0.3
	Eritrea	improved	1.6	1.0
	Ethiopia	improved	4.3	3–4
	Mozambique	improved	1.0	0.4

CIA credit for having changed, although they changed because the cold war ended. It ended largely because Russia and East Europe developed an educated middle class which was no longer supportive of a no-choice monopolistic political system and economy.

A key reason for presenting these data and the analysis of the world trouble spots is that the Developmental Policy Studies Consortium is interested in conducting win–win analysis workshops in them. The Consortium consists of representatives from about 50 countries who are interested in the application of social science to improving the quality of life in developing nations. Time and resources are scarce and should be used where the need is greatest and where they might be able to make a difference. The Consortium workshops are conducted for professors, government officials and journalists who are interested in resolving policy disputes in their countries and especially in win–win resolution. This is in contrast to the lose–lose situations which have existed in many of these countries, where virtually every major group is worse off as the result of bad policy decisions, rather than better off because of win–win policy decisions.

Social Indicators

The data presented in Table 3.1 are organized by country and cover people at risk, food, politics, the environment, facilities and health.

Trends

The data in Table 3.2, again organized by country, indicate the level of intensity of the various conflicts and emergencies, the trend as regards the evolution of the humanitarian situation and the number of people in need.

4 Postwar Developments: Bosnia and Public Policy

Basic Concepts

Bosnia

Bosnia has many policy problems, as well as other countries in the world. We are talking primarily about post-war problems, not so much the problem of how to bring the war to a close. We are assuming that the war is closed now that Serbia is no longer supplying the Bosnian Serbs and the Bosnian government has the upper hand.

It is frequently argued that a peace treaty (rather than just the present ceasefire) is needed before Bosnia can develop policies for its economy, technology, society, polity and legal systems. That may be partly true, but it is also true that having plans for the development of Bosnia can help bring about a ceasefire and then a peace treaty. Such plans can give stronger motivation or justification for ending the shooting.

Applicability Elsewhere

The ideas expressed in this chapter are expressed in terms of Bosnia, partly because it is one of the world's most violent trouble spots as of 1995. However, the ideas are widely applicable to other trouble spots, such as the following, presented in alphabetical order:

1 Africa, including Angola-Mozambique, Liberia, Rwanda-Burundi, Somalia and Western Sahara.
2 Asia, including China, India, the Middle East and Pakistan. The Middle East includes Egypt, Iran, Iraq, Israel, Jordon, Kuwait, Lebanon, Libya, the Palestinian Authority and Syria.
3 Eastern Europe, including the Caucusus, Moldova and Tajikistan. The

Caucusus includes Abkhazia, Armenia, Azerbaijan, Chechnya, Georgia and Ossetia.
4 Latin America, including Bolivia, Brazil, Central America, Columbia, Haiti, Mexico and Peru. Central America includes El Salvador, Guatemala, Nicaragua and Panama.

The ideas are also applicable to developing and industrialized nations in general, since the ideas touch upon important policies such as the following.

1 Economic policy, including unemployment, inflation, growth, training, technologies, exports, competition, capital, factories, agriculture, labor and business consumers. These policies are directed towards the overall goal of prosperity.
2 Social policy, including population, schools and poverty. These policies are directed toward merit treatment and training the young.
3 Engineering and science policy, including pollution, housing, land use, energy, health and technological innovation. These policies are directed toward technological goals such as inexpensive energy to increase productivity and improved medical technology to increase longevity.
4 Political policy, including branches of government and party systems. The branches of government are especially useful in carrying out the majority will aspect of democracy. The party systems are especially useful in enabling minority viewpoints to try to convert the majority.
5 International relations, including world peace and international trade.
6 Legal policy, including crime reduction, criminal justice, anti-discrimination and freedom of speech and religion.

In light of the above, a developing nation might be defined as a nation that scores relatively low on a composite index. The above six public policy fields can be used to develop that index. A trouble spot might be defined as a nation that is in an emergency state, especially in economic policy and/or external political policy. Trouble spots can be economic if their prosperity level is below a minimum threshold. They can also be political if their participatory activity is below a certain level. This chapter is concerned with means of raising these levels for developing nations, trouble spots and other places in general.

Economic Policy

Unemployment, Inflation and Growth

Bosnia needs to push for economic growth more than most countries. It has stagnated or even undergone negative growth during the first half of the 1990s. There will probably be some funding available from the United States, the World Bank and the European Community. Thus the question becomes, not so much where to get money to finance appropriate policies for dealing with unemployment, inflation, the deficit, and economic growth, but how the money should be spent. The type of spending that is most relevant for economic growth is that for training and technology.

Bosnia needs to spend money on organizing its educational institutions better. That is a long-run prospect if we are talking about elementary school, high school and college. Bosnia needs training of workers to deal with new technology now, meaning on-the-job (OJT) training. The business firms are in bad shape with regard to funding such activities. Outside money is needed. The Department of Labor, meaning Bob Reich, could send one or more experts on setting up OJT (on-the-job training) programs.

There may be urgent need for someone from the Office of Technology Assessment to talk about what new technologies Bosnia especially needs and where they can come from. The new technologies may relate to transport, communication, manufacturing, energy and agriculture, which calls for a lot of expertise. Each area means a different person from a different US department, such as the DOT (Department of Transportation), FCC (Federal Communications Commission), Department of Commerce, Energy and Agriculture, as well as specialists from AID (Agency for International Development). Communicating with these experts may mean sending fax letters and making phone calls, as the regular mail may take too long. The *Government Organizational Manual* gives phone numbers and fax numbers. The Developmental Policy Studies Consortium can call the office of the head of each department and ask who or what unit might be most relevant to advising on new technologies in each of these areas for the reconstruction of Bosnia.

Later there will be a need for Bosnia to have exportable products. For now, whatever is produced may need to be absorbed within the economy. Later there may also be a need for government capital. For the time being, the government has been putting all its extra money into defense. It has virtually no money available internally. Later the government can push for more competition in various industrial sectors, but for the present reconstruction crisis means that this cannot be undertaken yet.

Sectors of the Economy

Regarding specific sectors of the economy, the Consortium may need to talk to a lot of knowledgeable people, asking what the situation is and then acting on ideas that will be suggested, as they have been in other places in the past. The sectors include factories, agriculture, labor and commerce. Bosnia may have a lot of state-owned factories, left over from the Yugoslavian socialistic system, and perhaps even some state farms. Rather than sell these factories and farms, the state should contract them out, either domestically to entrepreneurs or to those who would like to come either to make money or to be helpful. They should not make the mistake of going overboard all at once in terms of privatization.

On the matter of agriculture, the food stamps idea works well in enabling farmers to get high prices as an incentive to produce, while at the same time enabling consumers to pay only low prices. In order to reimburse the farmers the state may have to show that they are doing things to improve their productivity, such as adopting new herbicides, pesticides, fertilizer, hybrid seeds and farm equipment. Likewise, labor consumers will have to show that they are improving their productivity in order to qualify for food stamps, such as being in a training program. Yugoslavia in the past was good at bringing labor and management together to plan more efficient production. They can also plan how to increase the total revenue of the firms, partly by improving quality and lowering prices. They also need to be concerned with workers who are displaced as a result of increased efficiency.

A third problem concerns relations between business and consumers. The most important businesses in that regard are energy and communications. From the start, these should be handled with multiple contracting out in order to encourage competition. The Yugoslavian system involved 100 per cent state-owned electric companies and state-owned telephone companies.

Social Policy

On the matter of social policy, there will be a need for population control, which means birth control information and devices. A welcome outcome of improved family planning would be a dramatic fall in the abortion rate. Abortions were a frequent form of birth control in communist countries. Availability of contraceptives was thought to lead to increased sexual activity that would interfere with worker productivity. As a result, most of Eastern Europe has an unnecessarily high abortion rate. Bosnia has not yet had an opportunity to have legal reform since the end of the cold war, since it went straight from a communist dictatorship into a war that has come to an end.

The schools system has yet to be straightened out. This means funding from general sources such as the national income tax, avoiding the mistake the United States has made of relying on local property taxes. It also means activities on the part of the national government to provide some minimum number of dollars per student for rural and urban students, and for low-income and middle-income students.

Poverty problems should be met by (1) economic growth, discussed earlier, (2) birth control as part of family policy and (3) a jobs program that applies especially to poor people on public aid. The jobs problem can also apply also to the elderly, the disabled, mothers of pre-school children and workers displaced by increased productivity and so on.

Engineering and Science Policy

Physical Planning

With regard to physical planning, as contrasted to social, economic and political planning, the latest technologies need to be adopted to reduce pollution. This is not a serious problem: getting the economy up and running (with employment and inflation down) is more important than clean air or water. The reason for showing any concern at all is that, if there is going to be a retooling with new technologies, now is the time to consider low pollution technologies, rather than having to retrofit or make changes later.

Housing needs to be privatized. Bosnia probably has more public housing than the United States has. It is a socialist republic in a former socialist country. It is not clear how much more socialist Bosnia was than Croatia, Serbia, Slovenia or the other republics of the former Yugoslavia. Bosnia was the poorest province, and thus probably more left-wing than Slovenia, which may have been the richest and most under the influence of Germany. The voucher system should be substituted for public housing in order to break up the concentration of low-income people and also to save the government money.

In this state of redevelopment and land use, there is a choice of where to build housing, factories and office buildings. The choice should be made in favor of some dispersion rather than concentrating so much in the central city, which makes for congestion and lots of commuting time. The fact that Bosnia (including Sarajevo) has been bombed provides something of a blank slate for building a new nation, with new economic, social, political and physical structures.

Science Policy

Physical and biological science policy deals with energy, health and technological innovation. For energy, the state will probably use coal and oil rather than anything very innovative. If they are getting enough money from the outside, they could look into second generation nuclear reactors, like those being built in Chernobyl and North Korea. On health care, they state should adopt a health maintenance organization (HMO) system with government partial subsidies to cover health insurance rather than socialized medicine, a single payer system or some kind of public aid like Medicaid. A single payer system involves the government paying for all medical costs by paying directly to the doctors or reimbursing the patients, as is done in Canada.

For technological *innovation*, a legal system should be adopted that rewards inventors by giving them an exclusive right to royalties and not a monopolistic patent. Bosnia is more receptive to these kinds of ideas than almost any other country. It is a country whose industrialization is above average – it is not a developing nation in Africa, Asia or Latin America. It has been devastated by a civil war and is open to new ideas. Bosnia has also been devastated by the transition from socialism to capitalism and dictatorship to democracy.

Political Policy

As for political reform, the country especially needs a semi-sovereign federalism, or at least a semi-autonomous system of federalism, so that the Serbian and Croatian provinces have some home rule and are not so likely to want to secede. The branches of government need stability, which means a presidential form. The courts should be given the independence to exercise judicial review, which means having judges appointed for life.

Single-member districts can encourage a two-party system. Public funding of campaigns can discourage special interests from bribing legislators. Also a nation can encourage high turnout with minimum double voting by using the invisible ink method employed in South Africa and other countries. There is a need for districting, with populations of equal size in each district. Bosnia could have three-member districts to provide minority representation, but this might be too complicated at first. It is worth suggesting, however, as there are minority ethnic groups in every part of the country. Districting refers to drawing electoral areas from which one or more representatives are chosen for a legislature.

International Relations

Once a peace treaty is signed, there should be no further peace problems: no outside country threatens Bosnia – its defense problems have largely come from within. Bosnia does need to be recognized as a sovereign state and a member of the United Nations. The United States, Western Europe, Russia and other countries should quickly send ambassadors to Sarajevo and accept ambassadors in return.

On the matter of international trade, Bosnia needs to develop products for export. Bosnia should be able to establish fruitful trade links with the other former republics of Yugoslavia and with neighboring countries, including Romania, Hungary, Poland, Greece, Italy, Germany and Switzerland. That includes all bordering countries in all directions, including the Czech Republic and Slovakia. Those countries can also sell to Bosnia, which means Bosnia needs to lower or wipe out its obstructive tariffs. There will be resistance to this, because of the need to promote the infant industries of Bosnia. The counterargument is that the people of Bosnia should be able to buy a lot of goods from nearby countries, including Serbia and Croatia.

Legal Policy

Legal Issues

Legal issues include crime reduction, courts, equal treatment and freedom of speech and religion. Many eastern European countries had a crime wave as a result of the breakdown in government authority. If Bosnia can get its economy going with low unemployment, there should be a lot less crime. Bosnia has plenty of jobs that need doing as part of the reconstruction activity. It will have money available for paying workers, given the outside funding. It does not have a serious drug problem or a gun control problem. It does have a poverty problem, but it is a poor country. It is not a poverty problem like that of the United States, which is a rich country that tolerates people living below a minimum level. Bosnia has been in a state of war, with many people living below a minimum level. When poverty is so widespread, it does not generate so much resentment. Inflation needs to be brought down, too, otherwise people may resort to crime in order to get money to meet the high prices.

There is a need to clarify the criminal justice system. A reasonable system is already in place, with police, courts and prisons. They probably do not need much in the way of reforms on those matters. Reforms might include right to counsel for the poor in criminal and civil cases. Bosnia operates under the Napoleonic code, which does not provide for jury trials. There should be a minimum due process recognized in all cases, including notice of wrongdoing, right to cross-examine one's accusers, right to bring one's own witnesses, right to appeal, right to have a judge who is not a complaining party and right to counsel. Right to counsel may at present just include right to hire counsel, with the local bar providing volunteer lawyers. The country may be too poor to provide salaried government attorneys. Appeals may also have to be limited to special cases.

Civil Liberties

The legal issues of equal treatment and freedom of speech and religion need to be singled out. Anti-discrimination legislation is especially necessary in a pluralistic society. Nobody should be discriminated against because they have a Serbian, Croatian, Muslim or other ethnic background. There should be no gender discrimination. There should also be no religious discrimination, but that is tied in with ethnic discrimination. Religious discrimination includes Roman Catholic (mainly Croatian), Russian Orthodox (mainly Serbian) and Muslin (mainly other Bosnians). There are also some Jews in Bosnia, including Sarajevo. They are mainly descendants of the Spanish and Portuguese exiles of 1492.

There is a need to guarantee (1) separation of church and state, (2) freedom of religion and (3) freedom of speech. This may be part of some constitutional drafting. If the Bosnians are going to start from scratch, they will need a constitution. The new constitution may include (1) political rights, like the US Constitution, (2) economic rights, like the Yugoslavian Constitution, and (3) new 21st-century rights, like the right to expect the government to promote economic growth and the right to expect the government to provide lifetime education and upgrading of skills.

The drafting of the constitution could be especially interesting. Bosnia has an opportunity to bring together its equivalent of the founding fathers to establish a new constitution. This would involve a convention, with representatives from all the provinces and big cities in the country, and perhaps some outside experts to serve as advisers, including constitutional law experts from the United States, such as Lawrence Tribe of Harvard Law School, and also people like John Nowak and Ronald Rotunda from the University of Illinois, both of whom have East European backgrounds and might be interested in participating.

Some Possible Next Steps

Bosnia

A lot needs to be done to develop public policy in Bosnia, including economic, technology, social, political and legal policy. A step in that direction might be the convening of a group of diverse government people, journalists and professors in Sarajevo for a win–win workshop. They could discuss the formulation and implementation of the general aspects of appropriate public policies. 'Appropriate' here might especially mean public policies that are capable of exceeding the best initial expectations of conservatives, liberals, Serbs, Croats, Muslims and those with other major viewpoints involved in the Bosnian controversies.

This is win–win public policy, whereby all major sides can come out ahead. The opposite extreme is the case where all sides come out worse off, as a consequence of the war. A win–win approach can also be contrasted to a compromising approach, whereby each side is expected to make some concessions for the collective good. Compromising is better than continued warfare, but it is not as rewarding as all sides more than achieving their original goals. Compromising may also be unrealistic in situations that are as emotionally charged as that of Bosnia.

Appropriate people for such a win–win workshop might include leading social scientists, journalists and government people from Zagreb, Belgrade and Sarajevo, as well as interested persons from other parts of Europe and elsewhere. The object would be to obtain and disperse a better understanding of win–win policy making and dispute resolution, and particularly to apply those ideas in the Bosnian context.

Applicability Elsewhere

If the suggested workshop can help to develop win–win thinking is Bosnia, it should be capable of stimulating such thinking in other places, which could include the trouble spots mentioned earlier in Africa, Asia, eastern Europe and Latin America. Such a workshop also has the potential for helping to resolve a variety of public policy disputes, including the policies also mentioned at the beginning of the chapter, dealing with economic, social, technology, political, international and legal policy. Such a workshop could be referred to as a workshop on international dispute resolution or an IDR workshop.

A key point to emphasize is that these workshops do not necessarily have on their agenda issues such as resolving the war in country X or resolving the Q policy controversy. Instead, they are concerned with the more general idea of resolving controversies in ways that can enable all major sides to come out ahead of their best initial expectations simultaneously. The participants can be encouraged to think along these lines and can then take back to their everyday interactions a new perspective on whatever important problems they are dealing with.

A good example is the workshop that was held at Chulalongkorn University in Bangkok, Thailand, in May 1992 at the height of the pro-democracy demonstrations. The workshop was attended by academics and government people who went away with some new perspectives that may have had some short- and long-term impact on themselves, their colleagues and their students. Related workshops were also conducted (1) at Beijing University and the People's University in China in May–June 1989 at the time of the events in Tiananmen Square, (2) at the University of Philippines in January 1990 at the time of the military insurrection, (3) in New Delhi and Bombay in December 1992 at the time of the burning of the mosque at Ayodha, and (4) at the Russian Academy of Sciences in December 1991 when the Soviet Union was dissolved.

No systematic follow-up study has been done on the impact of these workshops on subsequent relevant decision making. There is an impact of political science on many legislators, administrators and judges around the world, not in the form of legislative testimony or insights into specific pending legislation, but by way of government decision makers having taken elementary political science courses in college or high school civics, where they learned basic ideas about branches of government, levels of government, political party systems, free speech, due process, civil service and so on. These ideas help shape the perspectives of conservative and liberal decision makers.

In that sense, the IDR workshops may not resolve international disputes on the spot, but they may plant the seeds for a way of thinking that may be conducive to resolving international and public policy disputes starting in the near or intermediate future after the workshops. Academics help train the decision makers. Journalists supply the decision makers with current information. The government people are the decision makers, or they interact with them. Thus these three sets of people are especially appropriate for participating in these IDR or win–win workshops in Bosnia and elsewhere.[1]

Notes

1. Relevant books dealing with Bosnia include Noel Malcolm, *Bosnia: A Short History* (New York University Press, 1991); Bogdan Denitch, *Ethnic Nationalism: The Tragic*

Death of Yugoslavia (University of Minnesota Press, 1994); Misha Glenny, *The Fall of Yugoslavia: The Third Balkan War* (Penguin Books, 1992) and Brian Hall, *The Impossible Country* (Godine Press, 1992). Relevant books dealing with public policy, especially from a win–win perspective, include Arnold Heidenheimer, Hugh Heclo and Carolyn Adams, *Comparative Public Policy: The Politics of Social Choice in America, Europe and Japan* (St Martin's, 1990); S. Nagel (ed.), *Encyclopedia of Policy Studies* (Marcel Dekker, 1994) and S. Nagel and Miriam Mills, *Developing Nations and Super-Optimum Policy Analysis* (Nelson-Hall, 1993).

PART II
POLICY ACROSS DEVELOPING NATIONS

5   Peace Studies and Research Centers

David W. Felder*

We know how to kill each other but not how to live together. Over a hundred universities have addressed themselves to this problem by instituting peace studies programs and new peace research institutes have been established, including the United States Institute of Peace, established by Congress. In this chapter I examine these developments.

Educating for Planetary Consciousness

One approach to peace studies, sometimes called global education, involves covering curriculum from many disciplines in a way that fosters a planetary consciousness. The movement to include the accomplishments of non-European cultures in the humanities curriculum has lately received publicity. At many universities, including Stanford, where students demonstrated for the change, humanities courses have been revised to make room for materials on Third World cultures.

Advocates of global education rate curricula according to whether or not they include materials on Third World cultures and nations (Latin America, Asia and Africa) and whether all viewpoints, including Third World viewpoints, are considered. Are alternative views of the causes of poverty and development considered? Do discussions of human rights include economic rights (for food, shelter, medical care, education, employment, etc.) in addi-

---

* EDITOR'S NOTE: Peace is perhaps the most interaction across either developing or industrial nations. As of 1997, the world has had no wars between sovereign nations since the Persian Gulf war. International hot and cold wars have been replaced by international trade. Internal wars though have increased, including wars between regional, ethnic, religious and ideological groups. Even they have recently decreased, partly as a result of increasing democracy and prosperity. More on those subjects in Chapters 6 to 9.

tion to civil and political rights? Does ecology include a discussion of ecological limits to economic growth, alternative attitudes we might take to our planet and how alternative lifestyles affect the planet? A global education aims at providing students with a background to deal with some of the global issues we face, such as the division between rich and poor nations, the conflicts over human rights and ecological problems.

Why is it important that students learn about the contributions of non-Europeans? Those who know only about European contributions to civilization are more likely to be racists. If one reads the writings of fascist and Nazi theorists, it is apparent that none of them ever learned anything about non-European cultures. One way we help people learn to live together is to encourage them to learn about each other.

Peace studies as a separate discipline, includes studying ways to minimize violence and examining alternatives to war and the issue of whether or not war is inevitable. In specific courses, students study methods of conflict resolution and learn about famous peacemakers such as the Reverend Martin Luther King, Jr. and Mohandas K. Gandhi.

Traditional education covers skills that people need in order to live together. By traditional education I mean a background in literature, the arts and the humanities: the kind of background that people refer to when they say that someone is 'well educated'. Such traditional standbys as introductory logic courses, that teach skills that help people either to agree or to understand why they are disagreeing, are essential to those who want to work for peace.

War and the Ability to Perceive Reality

An education for living with others include knowledge of self, of others, of how others see us and of how others see themselves. Several wars started because people lacked knowledge in these four areas, among them World War I. When Kaiser Wilhelm II of Germany heard that the Austrian crown prince, Franz Ferdinand, had been assassinated on 28 June, 1914, he thought that this act was a threat to all monarchies. If he had known himself better, he would have realized that he was misinterpreting a Serbian patriot's actions because of his own insecurities. The Kaiser then assumed that Czar Nicolas II, also a monarch, would welcome action to punish the 'assassins of royalty'. The Kaiser sent a letter to the Austrians promising 'faithful support' if they took punitive action against Serbia. He did not understand how either the Austrians or the Russians would perceive his actions. The Austrians invaded Serbia. The Czar interpreted this as an action against all Slavic people, rather than an action to protect monarchy. Russia entered the war in defense of Serbia. Because Kaiser Wilhelm had promised to support Austria, not understanding what Austria would do or what the Russian reaction would be, Germany found itself at war with Russia. Each side knew so little about the other that each thought the war would be over in a few weeks.

History is replete with such examples. Before the Korean War, in January 1950, Secretary of State Dean Acheson said in a speech that Korea was 'outside the US defense perimeter'. That statement was interpreted by the North Koreans as an invitation to cross the border with impunity.

Saddam Hussein's invasion of Kuwait may well have been prompted by a misunderstanding of statements made by US officials. On 24 July, 1990, nine days before Iraq's invasion of Kuwait and with Iraqi troops massed on Kuwait's border, Secretary of State James Baker's official spokesperson, Margaret Tutwiler, stated, 'We do not have any defense treaties with Kuwait, and there are no special defense or security commitment to Kuwait'. On 25 July the American ambassador to Iraq, April Glaspie, told Saddam Hussein that 'we have no opinion on the Arab-Arab conflicts, like your border disagreement with Kuwait'. The last statement is according to minutes of that meeting released by Iraq and not disputed by the Untied States. These statements might well have given Saddam Hussein reason to think that the United States would not come to the aid of Kuwait. Secretary Baker stated on NCB's 'Meet the Press' (23 September, 1990) that the statements by Tutwiler and Glaspie 'had to do with taking sides on a border dispute, not taking sides on the question of unprovoked aggression'. Had we understood better how Saddam Hussein might understand our statements and let it be clearly known how we would react to an invasion, Iraq might not have invaded Kuwait.

Many wars might be avoided if we understood better how people in other nations understand our actions. The United States misjudged the chances of winning support in Vietnam. The Vietnamese fought the French for 25 years. Whatever the stated goals of the United States in Vietnam, how could anyone think that the Vietnamese would see the United States as anything but another colonial power?

How can people learn to see accurately themselves, others, and how others see themselves? Studying alternative philosophies has been the traditional method. Studying different philosophies, one learns to trace the implications of the alternative premises that people accept. To do this successfully, one must suspend one's own belief system and try to fit into the thinking of others. One also sees how various thinkers have misunderstood each other. This is one of the most challenging and rewarding experiences a person can have and guarantees growth in one's ability to understand other people.

Peace Studies Programs

There are over 200 peace studies programs in US universities, most of which were started during the 1970s. Several good guides to these programs exist. *Peace and World Order Studies: A Curriculum Guide*, provides actual course syllabi under such headings as: alternative world order; international organization and law; economic development and well being; human rights and ecological balance. *The Guide to Careers and Graduate Education in Peace Studies* claims that graduate programs fall roughly into six areas: peace and justice in the religious context; general peace and conflict studies; conflict resolution; citizen participation in socioeconomic development; arms control and international security; and public interest law and/or alternative dispute resolution.

The authors of the *Guide to Careers* and many other writers on peace education, such as Betty A. Reardon, differentiate between negative peace and positive peace in their descriptions of peace education. According to Reardon, 'Most recent teaching has focused on negative peace – that is, on reducing the likelihood of war. It has emphasized the problems posed by arms races and specific cases of international conflict and it falls within what I classify as the reform approach to peace education. However, although the wider emphasis is on negative peace and the focus is on the problem of armed conflict, the subject of study is not so much *war* as *wars*. Most current peace education does not address war as an institution. She goes on, 'Positive peace has become the concept connoting a world in which the need for violence has been significantly reduced, if not eliminated. The major areas of concern in the domain of positive peace are the problems of economic deprivation and development; environment and resources; and universal human rights and social justice. Peace education seems to have subsumed all these areas into the general concept of global justice'.

Every person involved in peace studies cannot be thoroughly informed on all aspects of the subject. Political science departments tend to have courses or programs related to international studies, the United Nations and other international institutions. Colleges of education tend to have programs in international education and intercultural studies. Philosophy, religion, history, economics, psychology, anthropology, English and sociology departments all have their own particular emphasis. Where a peace studies program is placed in an educational curriculum depends on the individuals interested in the program and the internal workings of the university. Courses tend to reflect the academic discipline of the individuals and groups involved.

As programs were initiated in the 1970s, interest grew in making peace studies a distinctive field. This interest assumed that peace encompassed a clearly defined area of knowledge – an assumption rejected by many today.

While the boundaries of peace studies cannot be clearly delineated, some areas definitely fall within its purview, such as conflict resolution. One can demonstrate that peace studies can make a unique contribution by showing the benefits of studying conflict resolution.

Peace education has found a place in the elementary and secondary school curriculum. Some excellent materials on how to handle conflict have been developed for elementary school children. Instruction in conflict resolution can make a difference in areas where children might otherwise be overwhelmed by gangs and violence. While the skills taught in peace studies are important on a global level, they are also important in our personal relationships.

Peace Research Centers

The real test of peace studies is whether scholars in this field make actual contributions to peace. Peace research centers have already made tremendous contributions to peace, among them the International Peace Academy, which helped in the historic Camp David Accords that ended the state of war between Egypt and Israel.

Action-oriented, the International Peace Academy has programs for practitioners in international relations and also aids universities. It tries to be relevant and useful by producing papers that are useful to people involved in current international conflicts.

In the Camp David discussions, both Egypt and Israel sent participants to the academy and, at their request the academy made up a simulation that helped Israelis and Egyptians discuss the disengagement of troops in the Sinai. The simulation, based on facts readily available from newspaper reports, required both sides to play through the steps of reaching an agreement. Israeli and Egyptian negotiators who took part in the academy's simulations learned how to reach the actual agreement on the withdrawal of Israeli troops. The plans worked out in the simulation, which involved having UN troops move in to provide a buffer, were actually used.

The United States Institute of Peace was created in 1984 with a mandate to expand knowledge about the nature of war and peace, to provide lessons from that knowledge in a form that can be used by decision makers and to help educate the American public on ways to increase the chances for peace. The institute was set up to be analogous to the National Endowment for the Humanities and the National Science Foundation and to operate like a public foundation. Funded grants already include 'new approaches to conflict management' in addition to traditional research and scholarship.

One institute that amateur scholars can participate in is the Peace Research Institute. In addition to other work, it publishes more than 500 abstracts of peace-related publications a month in the *Peace Research Abstracts Journal*. The work of abstracting, done by volunteers from around the world, is interesting and important.

One final organization is an umbrella group that provides information on all peace research and education organizations. Founded in 1970, the Consortium on Peace Research, Education, and Development (COPRED) publishes *Peace Chronicle* and *Peace and Change* in which it reviews publications, provides information on peace studies programs and informs readers about grants and conferences related to peace.

6 Mini-symposium on Inter- and Intranational Dispute Resolution

International dispute resolution refers to ending a disagreement among national groups, especially an actual or potentially violent one. Such groups of individuals include countries, sub-units within countries, quasi-colonies or other entities whose disagreements have international implications. Super-optimum solutions refer to resolutions which can enable all sides or viewpoints to come out ahead of their best initial expectations simultaneously.

This chapter deals with six kinds of international disputes: those between (1) sovereign nations, such as the arms control dispute between the United States and the Soviet Union; (2) controlling countries and their colonies or quasi-colonies, such as the dispute between the United States and the Philippines over the military bases; (3) central governments and secessionist provinces, such as the dispute over the secession of Chechnya from Russia, or related problems in other Caucuses countries; (4) national or ethnic groups within a country, such as the Serbs and Croats within Yugoslavia, or Moslems and Hindus in India; (5) economic class conflict with international implications, such as land reform and rural guerrillas in the Philippines; and (6) pro-democracy uprisings such as those in Thailand in 1992 or China in 1989. All six types of disputes can lend themselves to super-optimum solutions. Doing so requires sensitivity to the methods and processes for generating SOS solutions, getting them successfully implemented and dealing with a multiplicity of missing information, constraints and goals.

As of summer 1997, some of these disputes have been resolved, but they were all active where and when the analyses were written and presented: the US–USSR problem, presented at the USSR Academy of Sciences in early December 1991; the problem of Philippines military bases presented at the College of Public Administration of the University of the Philippines in January 1991; Chechnya presented at the Russian Academy of Sciences in late December 1991; the problem of the former Yugoslavia, presented at the University of Zagreb in 1987 and 1992; land reform, presented in the *Pakistan Journal of Rural Development and Administration* in 1992; and Thailand democracy, presented at Chulalongkorn University in May 1992, and Tiananmen Square, presented at the People's University and Beijing University in May–June 1989. The main dispute that still needs to be resolved is between the democratic and dictatorial viewpoints in China.

Disputes between Sovereign Nations

Bilateral arms reduction stemming from the Reagan–Gorbachev agreements exceeds the liberals' best expectations since liberals had been pushing for a freeze as a radical left-wing alternative to increased arms build-up. The idea of a drastic reduction clearly goes beyond a mere freeze. Bilateral arms reduction exceeds the conservatives' best expectations since it has been accompanied by a reduction in the threat from the Soviet Union, rather than an increase. The reduced threat could mean a substantial increase in funds available for improving the American economy, which both conservatives and liberals should welcome.

A Joint Perspective

This kind of analysis is shown in Table 6.1. The alternatives as of about 1985 were as follows:

1 a conservative alternative of a nuclear arms build-up and the Strategic Defense Initiative (Star Wars);
2 a liberal alternative of a unilateral freeze or disarmament;
3 a neutral alternative of conventional arms development;
4 an SOS alternative of bilateral arms reduction.

The goals of both the United States and the Soviet Union were:

1 the conservative or nationalistic goal of avoiding being conquered and preferably conquering the other side;
2 the liberal or pacifist goal of avoiding nuclear war;
3 the neutral goal of reducing the burden on the economy;
4 a second neutral goal of being politically feasible.

The relations between the alternatives and the goals are shown on a 1–5 scale: 5 means highly conducive to the goal, 4 means mildly conducive, 3

Table 6.1 Evaluating policies toward arms control

Criteria Alternatives	C Goal Avoid being conquered C=3 L=1	L Goal Avoid nuclear war C=1 L=3	N Goal Less burden on economy C=2 L=2	N Goal Politically feasible C=2 L=2	N Total (neutral weights)	L Total (liberal weights)	C Total (conservative weights)
C Alternative Nuclear arms build-up and SDI	4.5	1	3	1	18	15	22.5
L Alternative Unilateral freeze or disarmament	2	4	3	3	24	26*	22
N Alternative Conventional arms development	3	3	2	3	22	22	22
SOS Alternative Bilateral arms reduction and conversion to civilian use	5	5	5	4	38	38**	38**

* = this is the highest total in the column before considering the SOS alternative.
** = this is the highest total in the column after considering the SOS alternative.

means neither conducive nor adverse, 2 means mildly adverse and 1 means highly adverse. The neutral totals involve giving each goal a middling weight or multiplier of 2 on a 1–3 scale. Thus the neutral totals simply involve adding the relation scores and doubling the sum.

The liberal totals involve giving the neutral goals a middling weight of 2. The liberal totals give the conservative goal a low weight or multiplier of 1 on a 1–3 scale and they give the liberal goal a high weight of 3 on the 1–3 scale. Thus the liberal alternative wins on the liberal totals before looking to the SOS alternative. The conservative totals also involve giving the neutral goals a weight of 2. The conservative totals, however, give the conservative goal a high weight or multiplier of 3, and the liberal goal a low weight or multiplier of 1. Thus the conservative alternative wins on the conservative totals before looking to the SOS alternative.

The SOS alternative of bilateral arms reduction does so well on all four goals that it exceeds the best that the conservatives previously offered using conservative goals and weights. It also exceeds the best that the liberals previously offered using the liberal goals and weights. Exceeding the best expectations of both conservatives and liberals is the essence of a super-optimum solution.

Two Separate Perspectives

Table 6.2 shows how the US–USSR arms control negotiations might be viewed as of 1990. Eight alternative positions are shown: four are alternatives of the USA, and four are alternatives of the USSR. Each side is faced with basically the same four alternatives:

1. Keep the arms situation as it is. This is the most conservative reasonable alternative as of 1990. It is no longer being actively proposed that the arms race should be increased.
2. Have a big reduction in arms. This is the new liberal alternative. It is interesting to note that liberals were formerly advocating a freeze, which is now in effect the conservative alternative. This is a good example of why yesterday's liberal sometimes becomes today's conservative.
3. Have a little reduction between (1) keeping things as they are and (2) a big reduction. This is logically the neutral or compromise position. It typically involves no innovative ideas, but merely splitting the difference between the conservative and liberal positions.
4. A super-optimum solution which could consist of a combination of a big reduction and various international trade agreements between the United States and the Soviet Union, or even more broadly between the United States plus western Europe and the Soviet Union plus eastern Europe.

Table 6.2 A super-optimizing perspective on US–USSR negotiations, 1990

		National security (C)	GNP (L)	Neutral totals	Liberal totals	Conservative totals
A	USA perspective					
(C)	As is	3	3	12	12	12*
(L)	big reductions	2	4	12	14*	10
(N)	little reductions	2.5	3.5	12	13	11
(S)	big reductions and trade	4	5	18	19**	17**
B	USSR perspective					
(C)	As is	3	3	12	12	12*
(L)	big reductions	2	4	12	14*	10
(N)	little reductions	2.5	3.5	12	13	11
(S)	big reductions and trade	4	5	18	19**	17**

* = this is the highest total in the column before considering the SOS alternative.
** = this is the highest total in the column after considering the SOS alternative.

The four alternatives which the Soviet Union is considering are virtually identical. It is often the case in bilateral dispute resolution that the two sides are faced with the same alternatives. They differ mainly regarding what their goals are. Inspection is no longer such a big issue as a result of increased openness on the part of the Soviet Union and improved surveillance technology. Afghanistan is no longer such a controversy in view of the Soviet withdrawal. Likewise, the United States has stopped giving military aid to the Nicaraguan rebels and it looks as if there will be a reasonably meaningful electoral process in both Nicaragua and Afghanistan.

On the matter of goals, there are basically only two, although they could be subdivided, and other lesser goals could be added. Since there are two goals on the part of the United States and two goals on the part of the Soviet Union, there are four goals altogether.

1 Promoting the national security of the United States. This is a relatively conservative goal. It is also endorsed by liberals, especially if the external threat is from a right-wing source, as in World War II, or even a dictatorial left-wing source as during much of the cold war.
2 Promoting the gross national product of the USA, including the idea of full employment and increased international competitiveness. This is a

relatively liberal goal, especially if full employment is emphasized, but one also strongly endorsed by conservatives, especially if the emphasis is on international competitiveness and reduced inflation.
3. Promoting the national security of the Soviet Union. This is definitely an important goal of the Soviet military and also the civilian government. Too often the American State Department takes the position that the Soviet Union has nothing to worry about from the United States. The more important position is not whether they have anything to worry about, but whether they perceive that they have something to worry about.
4. Promoting the gross national product of the Soviet Union. This is also definitely an important goal of the Soviet Union, especially the civilian government and the civilian population. Too often the CIA and people in the State Department take the position that the Soviet Union does not care about consumer goods and raising living standards. It is obvious at least since 1988 (if not before) that people in the Soviet Union and eastern Europe do want a better quality of life in terms of both economic goods and political accountability.

Table 6.2 shows how US and the USSR negotiators are likely to perceive the relations between each alternative and each goal. The relations are expressed on a 1–5 scale: a 5 means that, if the alternative increases, the goal is likely to increase greatly; 4 means that the goal is likely to increase slightly; 3 means that the goal is not likely to increase or decrease; 2 means that the goal is likely to decrease slightly; and 1 means that, if the alternative increases, the goal is likely to decrease greatly. If the first alternative is to keep things as they are, that is likely to have no change on either national security or the gross national product. Therefore a 3 is inserted in the first two cells in the top row for both the USA and the USSR. If the second alternative is to have a big reduction in arms, that is likely to be perceived as causing at least a slight decrease in national security by the USA and by the USSR. The funds that might be released from such a reduction, however, are likely to be perceived as being capable of increasing the GNP of the USA and the GNP of the USSR by using those funds to develop and diffuse new technologies that will increase each country's economic capabilities.

The third alternative of a small reduction scores a 2.5 on national security, between the 3 of doing nothing and the 2 of a big arms reduction. Likewise, a small reduction scores 3.5 on GNP, between the 3 of doing nothing and the 4 of a big arms reduction. Like a typical compromise, it achieves the worst and the best of both of the other alternatives. As a result, it generates about the same total score. All three of the traditional alternatives generate total scores of 6 for both the Unites States and the Soviet Union. That means they are all about equally undesirable or equally desirable. The compromise alternative, however, is more likely to be adopted because it scores higher on the unshown goal of political feasibility. It is more politically feasible because both conservatives and liberals will vote for it as a second choice. They will then console themselves by saying that things could have been worse if the other side had won.

Under a super-optimum solution, both sides do win, and they can win even better than their initial best expectations. At first glance, one might question how a big reduction plus trade can result in more national security than a big reduction alone. That implies that national security is only dependent on how well armed each country is. A country that has a lower GNP than it could have may be weakening itself regarding arms capability and the ability to fight a war. More important, trade between two countries who might otherwise be hostile can create a mutually beneficial interdependence that decreases the likelihood of hostile interaction. Good examples include the unwillingness of the Reagan administration to punish the Soviet Union for its invasion of Afghanistan by prohibiting grain shipments, or the unwillingness of the Bush administration to punish China for its suppression of the pro-democracy movement by invoking trade sanctions. In both cases, the supposedly less anti-Communist liberals were more likely to favor the grain embargo and trade sanctions, partly because they are less sensitive to the value of international business transactions. In other words, active trading between the United States and the Soviet Union can do more to decrease the likelihood of their going to war and thus to increase their national security than either an arms increase or an arms decrease. This explains the 4 in the SOS row of the national security column.

The 5 in the SOS row of the GNP column reflects the fact that a big reduction alone generates a relation score of a 4 by virtue of the funds that are released from arms development to be available for supply-side economics, industrial policy and the development of new technologies. It is no coincidence that, among the top industrialized countries of the world, Japan and West Germany now score the highest in productivity increases and the lowest in arms expenditures per capita. The United States and the Soviet Union score the highest in arms expenditures per capita, while they score the lowest in recent productivity increases. In addition to the effect on GNP of the big arms reduction, the SOS also produces a positive effect by virtue of the trade agreements between the west and the east. One might say that the United States does not need the Soviet Union as a trading partner. For that matter, one could say that the United States could survive with no outside trading partners, and maybe the Soviet Union could do. If both countries want to improve their living standards substantially, however, they should take advantage of their potential abilities to buy and sell products from each other. The Soviet Union is one of the leading grain buyers of the world and could be a leading buyer in almost any field, given the size of its population. The Soviet Union is one of the leading producers of oil and gold, and it could become a leading producer in other fields if it concentrated its resources on what it can do relatively well, the way Japan has. The United States could sell grain and other products to the Soviet Union in return for gold, oil and other products, thereby easing the international deficit which can be paid in gold and the US energy problems.

Everything that is shown in Table 6.2 can be subjected to a computerized 'what if' analysis. Such an analysis enables one to determine what it would take to bring any of those alternatives that are tied for second place up to first place. It also enables one to determine the effects of adding additional goals, changing the alternatives or changing any of the inputs. That kind of 'what if' capability may be the most important purpose that is served by working with decision-aiding software. Some of the benefits can also be obtained by working with a spreadsheet matrix (like that of Table 6.2, with alternatives, goals, relations and total scores) even if the matrix is not computerized. One type of sensitivity analysis that is often especially helpful is to ask what would be the winning alternative if we just concentrated on the conservative goals or gave them extra weight, which in this case would be national security. Likewise, what would be the winning alternative if we just concentrated on the liberal goals or gave them extra weight, which in this case would be having a higher GNP with full employment and lots of consumer good? One exciting characteristic of super-optimum solutions is that they win even when one only uses conservative weights or when one only uses liberal weights. The reason here, and often in other SOS situations, is that the SOS alternative does better than the other alternatives on every individual goal, not just better on the overall total. There are ways of systematically arriving at super-optimum solutions: see S. Nagel and M. Mills, 'Generating Super-Optimum Solutions', in Marc Holzer (ed.), *Public Productivity Handbook* (Marcel Dekker, 1992).

Disputes between Controlling Countries and Colonies or Quasi-colonies

The problem of American military bases in the Philippines is an especially challenging one. Problems, in order to qualify as SOS problems, need to have the following characteristics.

1   There should be at least one conservative alternative and at least one liberal alternative. If there is only one alternative for dealing with the problem, there is no problem since there is no choice, although one

could say that there is still a go/no-go choice as to whether that one alternative should be adopted.
2 There should be at least one conservative and at least one liberal goal. If all the goals are conservative, the conservative alternative should win easily. Likewise, if all the goals are liberal, the liberal alternative should win easily.
3 The conservative alternative should do better on the conservative goal, with the liberal alternative doing better on the liberal goal. That is the tradeoff requirement. If either alternative does better on both kinds of goals, that alternative should win easily.
4 It should be possible to say meaningfully that conservatives give relatively more weight to the conservative goals and relatively less weight to the liberal goals, and vice versa for the assigning of weights by liberals. If that is not so, it is not so meaningful to talk about a conservative total with conservative weights and a liberal total with liberal weights.
5 There should be a super-optimum solution that does better than the previous conservative alternative on the conservative totals with conservative weights, and also does better than the previous liberal alternative on the liberal totals with liberal weights. This is the most difficult of the five characteristics to achieve, but it is still manageable.

The problem of what to do about the American military bases in the Philippines is especially difficult because it goes beyond the usual dilemma

Table 6.3 The Philippine–US military bases

Alternatives	C Goal Conservative concerns	L Goal Liberal concerns	L Goal Sovereignty	N Total (neutral weights)	L Total (liberal weights)	C Total (conservative weights)
C Alternative Bases and more money	4	3	2	18	19	17*
L Alternative No bases	2	3	4	18	23*	13
N Alternative Phase out	3	3	2	16	18	14
S Alternative Bases and massive credits to upgrade economy	5	5	3	26	29**	23**

* = this is the highest total in the column before considering the SOS alternative.
** = this is the highest total in the column after considering the SOS alternative.

of choosing between a liberal alternative that clearly wins with liberal weights, and a conservative alternative that clearly wins with conservative weights. An analysis of Table 6.3 tends to show that the liberal alternative barely squeaks by the conservative and neutral alternatives on the liberal totals, and the conservative alternative barely squeaks by the other two alternatives on the conservative totals. We thus have an even tighter dilemma than usual between the liberal and consumer alternatives.

The Alternatives

Working backward from those totals to the alternatives, the conservative alternative is basically to allow the American bases to remain, but to ask for more money. The liberal alternative is to throw the bases out. The neutral alternative is something in between, generally a gradual phasing out of the bases. Other in-between positions might involve throwing out the Clark Air Base but keeping the Subic Naval Base, or vice versa. Another possibility is to allow the bases, but with more flying of Philippine flags at the bases, together with other symbols of Philippine sovereignty. A recently arrived at middling position is allow the bases, but to give the Philippine government more say in how the planes should be used, especially with regard to putting down an attempted coup.

The phasing out idea is probably the most common middling alternative, but it blends into both the conservative and the liberal alternatives. The conservatives are willing to tolerate the bases, but they are going to be phased out eventually to some extent anyhow as the cold war decreases even further. They are also going to be phased out to some extent because they have probably already become rather obsolete in light of modern defense technology. Few if any of the planes or ships could ever get anywhere without being destroyed by modern missiles. The Russian equivalent of nuclear-armed Trident submarines in the Pacific Ocean could probably wipe out both the naval base and the air base almost before the alarm could ring. There are also bases elsewhere that are more welcome in nearby South Korea and Okinawa.

Likewise, the liberal alternative of throwing out the bases would have to be phased: they cannot be thrown out within a matter of hours. For one thing, the liberal and conservative members of the Philippine House of Representatives would not tolerate a rushed departure without allowing for substitute employment opportunities and some substitution for the large amounts of money that are spent by Americans associated with the bases. The Philippine Senate is elected with the whole nation as its constituency and is therefore not so sensitive to constituency pressures from Luzon, where the bases are located.

One might therefore think that there is really only one alternative here, namely to phase out the bases. This problem, however, illustrates the importance of symbolism and language in political controversy. Whether the liberals really mean it or not, they talk about throwing out the bases now, not phasing them out. Whether the conservatives really mean it or not, they talk about retaining the bases indefinitely. Thus the controversy needs to be resolved in terms of what each side argues, not necessarily in terms of the realities beneath the surface. Perceptions, value judgments and symbolism are often more important in resolving political controversies than empirical reality, especially in the short run.

The Goals

As for goals, Table 6.3 lists the first goal as 'Liberal concerns', which means a whole set of interests that liberals are especially sensitive to, including workers rather than employers, consumers rather than merchants, tenants rather than landlords, small farmers and businesses rather than big farmers and businesses, debtors rather than creditors, minority ethnic groups rather than dominant ethnic groups, and in general the relatively less well-off segments within society. The second goal is listed as 'Conservative concerns', which means a set of interests to which conservatives are especially sensitive, including employers, merchants, landlords, big farmers, big businesses, creditors and dominant ethnic groups. One useful aspect of this problem is that it goes to the heart of liberal versus conservative interests and constituencies, as contrasted to problems with lower impact.

The third goal is national sovereignty. In some contexts, such as when Russia nationalists talk about restraining the Lithuanians, expelling the Jews or otherwise discriminating against citizens of the Soviet Union who are not ethnic Russians, this can be a conservative goal. In other contexts, sovereignty can be a liberal left-wing goal, as where the Vietnamese have advocated becoming independent, from China, France, Japan, France again, the United States and China again, at various points in Vietnamese history. Likewise, it is a liberal concept in the Philippines when Filipinos talk about getting rid of the Spanish colonialists or the American imperialists, including what they consider to be military base imperialism. That makes sovereignty in this analysis a relatively liberal goal. Obviously, the goal of conservative concerns is a conservative goal, and the goal of liberal concerns is a liberal one.

Scoring the Relations

As for scoring the relations of the alternatives on the goals, both the liberal and conservative concerns are to some extent favorably affected by the present and additional American dollars. Those dollars benefit both workers and employers, consumers and merchants, tenants and landlords, small and large farmers, small and large businesses, debtors and creditors, and both minority and dominant ethnic groups. The amount of money is quite substantial. The Philippines is one of the top three recipients of American foreign aid in the world, along with Israel and Egypt, whose aid is lessening. The liberal and conservative concerns, however, do not benefit equally. The American presence has a conservative influence. The United States tends to be supportive of conservative pro-American politicians, especially in a country that has American military bases, such as South Korea, Greece, Turkey, West Germany, Spain and the Philippines.

To be more specific, the conservative alternative of retaining the bases with even more money is a neutral outcome or a 3 on a 1–5 scale with regard to liberal concerns. The money is at least a 4 on liberal concerns, but the conservative influence of the United States is a 2 or lower. Those two sub-scores average a 3. On the conservative concerns, the conservative alternative of the bases and more money gets at least a 4. On sovereignty, the conservative alternative is at least a 2 on a 1–5 scale, which is the equivalent of a –1 on a –1 to +2 scale.

The liberal alternative also produces a neutral 3 on liberal concerns. It gets a 4 with regard to getting rid of some of the American conservative influence, but it gets a 2 on losing the American money. The liberal alternative of no bases gets a 2 or lower on conservative concerns. It does relatively well on sovereignty, as both liberals and conservatives can recognize, although they may disagree on the relative weight of sovereignty in this context.

The neutral phase-out approach does about middling on liberal concerns. It provides some money for a while, which is good, but not as good as a lot of money for a long time. It provides a diminishing of American conservative influence, but not as fast as the liberals would like, and not as slow as the conservatives might like. By allowing the Americans to retain the bases even under a phase-out arrangement, the neutral alternative does not have a negative effect on Philippine sovereignty, although not as negative as the conservative alternative. We could show that difference by giving the neutral alternative a 2.5 on sovereignty or the conservative alternative a 1.5. Either way, the overall results are not affected.

A Super-optimum Solution

These overall results are that the liberal alternative wins on the liberal totals and the conservative alternative wins on the conservative totals, although not by much, as previously mentioned. Finding a super-optimum solution may be especially difficult where the alternatives are so nearly tied and where the problem is so filled with emotional symbolism. A possible super-optimum solution would involve two key elements: the first is a recognition (as much as possible on all sides) that the bases are probably going to be phased out in the future. This will not be due to the United States surrendering or to the Philippines overcoming the US opposition. It will be more due to defense technology changes (as mentioned above) that make these bases about as meaningful as the Maginot Line in France in 1940, Pearl Harbor in the United States in 1941 or the Singapore guns pointing to the sea in 1942. The phasing out will also be due to recent world changes that seem greatly to decrease the likelihood of a world war between the Soviet Union, eastern Europe and China, on the one hand, and the United States and its allies on the other.

More important than a natural rather than a forced phase-out is a second key element of a possible super-optimum solution. This element emphasizes massive credits to upgrade the Philippine economy. It could involve no payment of cash whatsoever on the part of the United States and yet provide tremendous economic benefits to the Republic of the Philippines. It involves a number of characteristics. First of all, the United States makes available an amount of credits that, when expressed in dollars, would be about twice as many dollars as the United States would be willing to pay in the form of rent or a cash payment. The United States would be willing to pay more in the form of credits for the following reasons:

1. It is normally a lot easier to give credit than to pay cash. An example might be returning merchandise to a store and asking for cash. One may receive various negative reactions as to why the merchandise should be kept. If, however, one asks for a credit slip, the decision maker is likely to be much more accommodating.
2. The American economy would benefit substantially if the credits could only be used in the United States to buy American products and services. That would benefit the United States more than paying out cash that is then spent in Japan or elsewhere. At the same time, it does not substantially hamper the Philippines in buying products and services needed to upgrade its economy.
3. The US economy would also substantially benefit indirectly from an upgrading of the Philippine economy, since that would enable the Philippines to buy even more American products and services in the future.

As for what the credits would be for, that is where the Philippines could especially benefit. The shopping list might include such things as the following:

1. credits to pay for personnel and facilities for on-the-job training and adult education to upgrade worker productivity;
2. relevant credits for upgrading Philippine higher education, especially in fields that relate to engineering and public policy which could have high marginal rates of return;
3. relevant credits for upgrading elementary and secondary education as part of a large-scale investment in human resource development;
4. relevant credits for seeds, pesticides, herbicides and farm equipment to make the land reform programs more successful, including the hiring of experts for training programs. Land reform in the Philippines is discussed below in Section V on 'Disputes between Conflicting Economic Classes with International Implications: Land Reform in the Philippines';
5. relevant credits for subsidizing suburban job opportunities, regional cities and overseas employment opportunities;
6. relevant credits to improve energy and electricity production in the Philippines, which is such an important aspect of improving the gross national product;
7. relevant credits for buying technologies that can improve productivity along with upgraded skills, including modern assembly line technologies;
8. relevant credits for health care and housing that can be shown to be related to increased worker productivity;
9. other credits for buying American products and services that relate to upgrading the Philippine economy, as contrasted to buying consumer goods or other products and services that have little increased productivity payoff.

There are additional benefits for both sides that should be mentioned. (By both sides in this context is meant the Republic of the Philippines and the United States.) Both sides also refer to the liberals and conservatives within the Philippines.

1. Providing credits rather than cash minimizes loss due to corruption. It is a lot easier to pocket money than it is to pocket a new schoolhouse or an expert consultant in on-the-job training.
2. Providing credits that are earmarked for upgrading the economy minimizes loss due to wasteful expenditures, including bureaucratic administration.
3. Waste is not going to be eliminated completely. We would not want a straitjacket system that discourages experimentation with innovative ideas for increasing productivity. If innovation is going to be encouraged, some waste must be expected, since not all innovative ideas work out well.

4 This could set a precedent for future American aid to other countries and future aid by other developed countries to developing countries. The key aspect of the precedent is emphasizing credits for upgrading the economy, as contrasted to an emphasis on food, shelter, clothing and other traditional charitable do-gooderism.
5 In that regard, we are talking about teaching people how to fish, rather than giving them a fish. The fishing analogy is endorsed by liberals who founded the Peace Corps and conservatives who believe in workfare rather than charitable handouts. Actually we are talking about teaching people how to develop and apply new technologies for doing such things as fishing, growing crops, manufacturing products, transporting, commuters and making public policy decisions. Workfare refers to enabling or requiring welfare recipients to obtain jobs.
6 The kind of programs that most win friends and influence people in favor of the United States might be those that involve bringing left-wing anti-Americans to the United States to receive training or having American trainers go to work with Philippine union leaders or Mindinao farmers. People acquire a much more favorable attitude toward Americans in that context than by receiving a sack of flour labeled 'Made in the USA'.

It might be noted that, if the Filipinos emphasize how obsolete the bases are becoming, they might succeed in getting rid of the bases faster. On the other hand, it might be wise to emphasize how valuable the bases are in order to get even more credits as payment for retaining them. On the third hand, the United States is not so unaware of the empirical realities, and it is not so unaware of bargaining techniques. This idea of retaining the bases along with an inevitable, at least partial, phase-out and massive credits for upgrading the Philippine economy should not be approached as a matter of traditional negotiation and game playing. Rather, it should be approached as a matter that can be resolved to the mutual benefit of all sides, in the sense of a super-optimum solution with all major viewpoints coming out ahead.

Disputes between Central Governments and Secessionist Provinces

Super-optimizing Applied to Russian Secession

Table 6.4 shows the application of SOS analysis to the problem of the proposed secession of Chechnya from the Russian Soviet Federated Socialist Republic (RSFSR). This application was developed in collaboration with Edward Ojiganoff, the Head of the Policy Analysis Division of the Supreme

Table 6.4 Secession of Chechnya from the RSFSR

Criteria Alternatives	C Goal Greater Russia and high RSFSR GNP	L Goal Chechnya independence and high Chechnyan GNP	N Total (neutral weights)	L Total (liberal weights)	C Total (conservative weights)
C Alternative Deny independence	3	1	4	5	7*
L Alternative Grant independence	1	3	4	7*	5
N Alternative More autonomy	2	2	4	6	6
S Alternative Economic union	≥2.5	≥2.5		≥7.5**	≥7.5**

* = this is the highest total in the column before considering the SOS alternative.
** = this is the highest total in the column after considering the SOS alternative.

Soviet of the RSFSR. The Chechnya problem is partly analogous to the proposed secession of Croatia from Yugoslavia or the secession of any ethnic region from a larger country of which it has been a part. The *alternatives* in the RSFSR–Chechnya situation are the following.

1 Deny independence to Chechnya. This can be considered the relatively conservative position because it seeks to conserve the country, state or political unit as it is.
2 Grant independence to Chechnya. This can be considered the relatively liberal position because it is more tolerant of dissident attitudes.
3 Retain Chechnya as a sub-unit within the RSFSR, but grant Chechnya more autonomy than it has at present. This can be considered the relatively neutral position.

The *goals* in the Chechnya situation are:

1 a key conservative goal is to favor greater Russia and seek a high national income for Russia;
2 a key liberal goal is to help Chechnya, including a high national income for Chechnya;
3 more goals, and possibly more alternatives, can be added later. For the sake of simplicity, however, we will begin with three basic alternatives and two basic goals.

The *relations* between those three alternatives and those two goals can be expressed in terms of a 1–3 scale. In that context, 3 means that the alternative is relatively conducive to the goal, 2 means neither conducive nor adverse and 1 means relatively adverse or negative to the goal. Relations can also sometimes be expressed in dollars, miles, 1–10 scales, question marks or other units.

Denying independence to Chechnya is perceived as being at least a mildly positive 3 on the goal of favoring greater Russia. Granting independence to Chechnya is perceived as being at least an undesirable 1 favoring greater Russia. More autonomy is in between 3 and 1, with a relatively neutral score of 2. On the other hand, granting independence to Chechnya is scored a 3 on the goal of helping Chechnya. Denying independence is scored a 1 on helping Chechnya. More autonomy is in between on that goal, with a neutral score of 2. Those perceptions and scores are likely to be approximately held by both conservatives and liberals in this context.

There are three *total scores* that can be generated from these data. The total scores are neutral, conservative or liberal, depending on the relative importance of the two goals. If the two goals are considered to be of equal importance, the neutral totals are 4 for each of the alternatives. If the conservative goal is considered more important than the liberal goal, we can count the conservative column twice. That results in totals of a 7 for denying independence ($3 + 3 + 1$), a 5 for granting independence ($1 + 1 + 3$) and a 6 for more autonomy ($2 + 2 + 2$). Thus, with conservative weights for the goals, the conservative alternative wins on the conservative totals.

Likewise, if the liberal goal is considered more important, we can count the liberal column twice. That results in totals of a 5 for denying independence ($3 + 1 + 1$), a 7 for granting independence ($1 + 3 + 3$) and a 6 for more autonomy ($2 + 2 + 2$). Thus, with liberal weights for the goals, the liberal alternative wins on the liberal totals. The single asterisk shows the winning alternative on each total column before the SOS alternative or super-optimum solution is taken into consideration.

Finding a Super-optimum Solution

The object is to find a super-optimum solution which will simultaneously win on the conservative totals over the conservative alternative and win on the liberal totals over the liberal alternative. That means being better than both the conservative best and the liberal best using their own goals and weights to judge what is best. In terms of the simple scoring system, such a solution needs to score positively or better than a neutral 2 on a 1–3 scale on both goals. That also means going above traditional tradeoff reasoning. The conservative alternative usually does well on the conservative goal, but not so well on the liberal goal. The liberal alternative usually does well on the liberal goal, but not so well on the conservative goal. The SOS alternative does at least mildly well on both goals.

Doing well on both goals does not require being a winner on each separate goal. It means being a winner on each of the two main totals. Those totals involve using conservative weights and liberal weights, respectively. If the suggested SOS alternative receives a 2.5 on each goal, then it will receive a 7.5 on the conservative total (2.5 + 2.5 + 2.5). That is higher than the 7 received by the conservative alternative. Likewise, the suggested SOS alternative will receive at least a 7.5 on the liberal total (2.5 + 2.5 + 2.5).

Developing an SOS alternative (which has those characteristics) requires a knowledge of the subject matter and some imagination. Finding such an alternative can be aided by the checklists which have been developed from previous case studies. See Nagel, *Creativity and Public Policy: Generating Super-Optimum Solutions* (Ashgate, 1998). Finding such alternatives can also be facilitated by decision-aiding software which makes use of multi-criteria decision analysis with a spreadsheet base. Such software is described in Nagel, *Decision-Aiding Software: Skills, Obstacles and Applications* (Macmillan, 1991).

A proposed SOS solution to the problem of Chechnya seceding from the RSFSR is to allow Chechnya its independence but as part of an economic union with the RSFSR and possibly other autonomous regions within the RSFSR and other neighboring political units. This is analogous to the RSFSR, the Ukraine and Belarus withdrawing from the USSR and forming an economic union or commonwealth. Such an economic union can benefit both the RSFSR and Chechnya by facilitating a profitable interchange of goods, capital, workers and ideas. It can later lead to developing a more meaningful division of labor than previously existed with the possibility of well-directed subsidies and incentives from the economic union to make the division of labor even more successful.

An alternative SOS might be to retain Chechnya within the RSFSR, but to seek to achieve the benefits of an economic union through immediate subsidies. Such an alternative may not be economically feasible from the perspective of the currently hard-pressed RSFSR. It may also be politically unfeasible from the perspective of the independence-seeking Chechnyas. To be a meaningful SOS requires satisfying the following five criteria:

1 the SOS must win on the conservative totals;
2 it must also win on the liberal totals;
3 it must win by a safe enough margin for the SOS to retain first place regardless of reasonable changes in scoring the relations between the alternatives and goals or in indicating the relative weights of the goals;

4 the SOS must be politically feasible so that it is capable of being adopted;
5 the SOS must be administratively feasible so that it is capable of being successfully implemented, including being backed by sufficient funding.

Disputes between Conflicting Nations within a Country

Super-optimizing Applied to Civil War in Yugoslavia

The above analysis can be applied to Yugoslavia through reasoning by analogy. Special points worth noting include the following.

1. Each republic and autonomous province of Yugoslavia could become a separate sovereign nation, or at least each republic could. They would each have a population and a national income that would be within a low to middle range among members of the United States.
2. They would be joined together in an economic union of six republics. This would be analogous to the joining of the seven former republics of the Soviet Union or the 12 nations in the European Economic Community. The so-called Eurasian Economic Union is more applicable since the members were formerly part of one country.
3. The new economic union could be referred to by such names as the Yugoslavia Economic Union or the South Europe Economic Union. The latter would allow for other southern European countries such as Greece to join. An alternative would be to have a Yugoslavia Economic Union consisting of the six Yugoslavian republics, but having the Yugoslavia Economic Union later join a larger economic union covering southern Europe or possibly central Europe.
4. The Yugoslavia Economic Union could add to its unity by having a constitutional monarchy as part of the union. The precedent for doing so is the former British Commonwealth. It is now the Commonwealth of Nations, but many of those nations still have a relation to Queen Elizabeth which gives them more unity, tradition and stability than they otherwise would have.
5. In the case of Yugoslavia, a democratic constitutional monarchy could serve a unifying peacemaking role. Crown Prince Alexander does evoke a favorable response from among many Serbs, Croats, Slovenes and other Yugoslavian ethnic groups. He probably evokes a more favorable response than the Yugoslavian national or federal presidency or other government institutions.
6. As of 1997, there are increasing case studies and experiences regarding the benefits and processes related to forming an economic union. Such

unions are becoming increasingly important in such places as western Europe, the former Soviet Union and the NAFTA pact among the United States, Canada and Mexico. As of 1997, however, there is increasing recognition of the need for retraining and other approaches to provide for disrupted workers and firms.

7. Moving ahead toward establishing such a union may make more sense in ending the civil war in Yugoslavia than trying to achieve a lasting ceasefire or a military solution.

8. The economic union can at first emphasize the unhindered exchange of goods, people, capital and ideas across all the boundaries of the former republics. It can also emphasize equality of opportunity for all ethnic groups in terms of equal treatment regardless of origins in matters of rights that relate to politics, criminal justice, education, employment, housing and consumers.

9. The economic union can later develop appropriate divisions of labor in terms of making the best use of the land, labor and capital of each former republic. That kind of division or specialization can be facilitated by well-directed subsidies and incentives available to the economic union.

10. Such an economic union is a super-optimum solution since it enables conservative nationalists and separatists to achieve more national identity and stature than they otherwise would have. At the same time, it satisfies the liberal emphasis on quality of life in terms of jobs and consumer goods.

11. It makes more sense than each country going off on is own without the benefits of the economic interaction associated with an economic union. It likewise makes more sense than forcing nations into a regional government above the member nations, or even a world government.

12. Some of these ideas are summarized in Table 6.5. It makes use of a 1–5 system of scoring relations rather than 1–3. It also uses a 1–3 system for weighting goals rather than 1–2.

13. These are general ideas with lots of potential for Yugoslavia in terms of peace, prosperity and political reform. They need to be further developed in collaboration with policy makers, political scientists, economists and other relevant people mainly in Yugoslavia.

14. The most appropriate next step may be to engage quickly but meaningfully in that kind of collaboration in order to develop and implement a worthwhile plan for creating a Yugoslavia Economic Union of six sovereign states. It could possibly include a constitutional monarchy as a peacemaking unifying force. It could bring together Serbs, Croats, Slovenes, Muslims, Albanians, Macedonians, Montenegrins and other Yugoslavians.

Table 6.5 International economic communities and super-optimum solutions

Alternatives	Criteria	C Goal National identity and stature C = 3 L = 1	L Goal Quality of life in terms of jobs and consumer goods C = 1 L = 3	N Total (neutral weights)	L Total (liberal weights)	C Total (conservative weights)
C	Alternative Nationalism and separatism	12 (4) 4	2 (2) 6	12	10	14*
L	Alternative One world of world government	6 (2) 2	4 (4) 12	12	14*	10
N	Alternative Regional government	9 (3) 3	3 (3) 9	12	12	12
S	Alternative Economic community	15 (5) 5	5 (5) 15	20	20**	20**

Notes:
1 The relations between each alternative and each goal are shown on a 1–5 relations scale or score in parenthesis. 5 means highly conducive to the goal; 4 means mildly conducive; 3 means neither conducive nor adverse; 2 means mildly adverse; 1 means highly adverse to the goal.
2 The conservative goal (C column 1) is given a weight or multiplier of 3 by conservatives (upper left-hand corner) on a 1–3 scale of weights, but a weight of 1 by liberals (lower right-hand corner).
3 The liberal goal (L column 2) is given a weight or multiplier of 1 by conservatives (upper left-hand corner), but a weight of 3 by liberals (lower right-hand corner).
4 A single asterisk shows the alternative that wins on the liberal totals (column 4) and the conservative totals (column 5) before considering the SOS alternative.
5 A double asterisk shows the alternative that wins after the SOS super-optimum solution is considered. The SOS should score higher than the former conservative winner on the conservative totals (column 5) and, simultaneously, higher than the former liberal winner on the liberal totals (column 4).

Post-Civil War Dispute Resolution
by Ivan Grdesic

This section is authored by Ivan Grdesic who as of 1997 is the head of the Political Science Department at the University of Zagreb in Croatia. He is also the former president of the Croatian Political Science Association and the East Europe Regional Coordinator for the Developmental Policy Studies Consortium. He speaks from an insider's perspective with regard to predictions and prescriptions for post-war former Yugoslavia. His section is written in response to Nagel's suggestion that Yugoslavia could maybe become an economic union, partly comparable to the commonwealth countries, with a figurehead monarch. Professor Grdesic's insider's perspective is followed by a brief reply from Nagel. This material provides a kind of interactive dialogue with regard to the resolving of a very real intranational and international dispute.

The situation in Croatia as of 1994 has changed. It does seem that the peace is holding and that UN forces will be sent to Croatia. Croatia is internationally recognized by more than 40 states (Russia too) and we hope that federal troops and the Serbian army will pull out from this region. Constitutional law on protection of the minorities has been passed and I hope it will be enforced.

It is now time to think about the future and in this general aim to maximize the greatest happiness ... I do agree with you. There are some elements that are now clearer than before. Republics of the former Yugoslavia are separate states. By the ruling of the arbitration expert commission of the Hague peace conference, there is no republic or state that can claim to inherit a Yugoslavia in the sense of international law. In this respect there is no provision for a Serbian king. And it must be emphasized that the idea of a monarchy would receive a favorable response only among Serbs. Princess Katherine of Serbia was in Belgrade in 1994 at the ceremony of the reconciliation between orthodox Serbian church in the country and in the exile for the first time after 1945. She was welcomed by the crowd, crying 'We want a/the king!' I can see in your comments to my letter that you have decided not to pursue this line of political integration. Now with the peace conference under Lord Carrington in Bruxelles I do not see the real need to have them call upon Bush and Yeltsin to call for a conference. I also doubt that Croatian politicians would agree to this kind of initiative.

I must say that I do not imply that doing anything "that might make queen and king look good that he is willing to have the war continue if the small price one has to pay is to give them some prestige for helping to end it." I am ready to pay a much bigger price to stop this war. But the problem is that there is no feasible way to use their goodwill without political implications. Royal family are not you and me that can be private persons. King and queen are always political figures and political figures bring opposition or support. Even more so when they publicly declare of being ready to come back and be the monarch of Serbia. And I think you still have the false impression that Croats and Slovenes have favorable responses toward them. I think that most of the people just do not care as long as this mater stays within Serbia.

There is no neutrality in the relationship between victim and aggressor. In this situation one can speak about neutrality only on an abstract level, ("overall utilitarian goal") and then one has to disregard causes and consequences of the conflict, take a long time perspective. If one rise high enough on abstract level there is for everything grounds for neutrality.

I must admit that it is really very hard to "go above traditional tradeoff reasoning." But than we are dealing more or less with the postwar situation and the economic cooperation will come one way or another, money is the strongest force. Under this presupposition we can work on SOS in economic terms: unhindered exchange of goods, people and capital. But not in the near future with the monetary union or central banking system. Right now the only economic issues between Serbia and Croatia, on both sides, are the war reparations and damage compensations.

The economic interest of Croatia toward Serbia and other less developed states of former Yugoslavia is to expand the market for industrial production, and that can be seen as neocolonialism as it was in the time of Yugoslavia. But real economic interest of Croatian service and tourism oriented economy is the economic integration with western states through regional integration such as "Alpe-Adria" and "Pentagonale" (Italy, Austria, Hungary, Slovenia, Croatia). So I see this only as one possible way of cooperation but probably not the primary one upon which one can built to much expectation. The best principal to provide enduring peace in this part of Europe is to recognize the existing borders, human rights and minority rights. I think I agree with Danica about the political side of this initiative. I am not willing to join any kind of project oriented to the establishing of any form (symbolic or "real") of (a) Yugoslavia (not even as a Yugoslav economic community), (b) introducing the Serbian royal family in the picture, and (c) approaching the problem in the neutrality attitude. I am willing to work on some form of post facto analysis that will be only this and not the platform for political initiative that I do not see as a viable option.

A BRIEF REPLY BY S. NAGEL I do not think I need to prepare a formal response since the above ideas are quite constructive in saying, 'we can work on SOS in economic terms: unhindered exchange of goods, people and capital, but not in the near future'. The most immediate issue is war reparations and damage compensation. But then comes the need to expand the market for industrial production of Croatia towards Serbia and other less developed states of former Yugoslavia, and especially Croatia towards Germany, Italy, Austria, Hungary and Slovenia.

What he may be saying is that he likes the idea of an economic community, but one based on Yugoslavia is too small, especially since Croatia is the most prosperous unit, although tied to Slovenia, and does not want to be supporting the 'other less developed states of former Yugoslavia'. He says that those other places might view Croatians taking the lead in an economic community as a form of neocolonialism. There is an element of snobbiness in this. I think the gulf between Croatia and Serbia is not exactly the same as the gulf between Britain and Uganda. It is about the same as the gulf between Illinois and Kentucky or Missouri. If Illinois sells products to Kentucky, they do not think that is neocolonialism.

On the other hand, Grdesic puts down Croatia's potential by overemphasizing tourism and service industries. Tourism can be a profitable business that does require sophisticated hotel management, but Croatia should have more to offer the world than some ancient museum places. Service industries are also capable of high technology. McDonald's uses the most advanced hamburger-making technology there probably is. Croatia is capable of getting into electronics and computers. The countries Grdesic mentions are not the big players. He did not specifically mention Germany. He mentions Italy, Austria, Hungary and Slovenia. Maybe he left Germany out because liberal Croatians like Grdesic have not forgiven Germany for the way it treated Croatia in World War II. The Croatians can learn some things from Germany, just as the Koreans, Chinese and Singaporeans have learned from Japan without having to like the way Japan treated them in World War II.

Disputes between Conflicting Economic Classes with International Implications: Land Reform in the Philippines

Table 6.6 provides an SOS analysis of land reform in developing countries, although it is especially based on the author's experiences in working with people from the Department of Agrarian Reform in the Republic of the Philippines. The table is a classic SOS table in that the rank order of the alternatives on the liberal totals are SOS, liberal, neutral and conservative. Likewise the rank order of the alternatives on the conservative totals are SOS, conservative, neutral and liberal.

The Traditional Inputs

More specifically, if we are talking about 100 units of land, the typical conservative approach tends to advocate retaining most of the ownership of the land in the hands of the traditional landed aristocracy. The typical liberal approach tends to advocate turning over most of the ownership of the land to landless peasants to farm. The typical neutral or compromise approach is something in between, although not necessarily exactly a 50–50 split of the 100 units.

Table 6.6 Land reform in developing countries

Criteria Alternatives	C Goal Productivity	L Goal Equity	N Total (neutral weights)	L Total (liberal weights)	C Total (conservative weights)

C Alternative
     Retain land
     (0 units)
	4	1	10	7	13*

L Alternative
     Divide land
     (100 units)
	1	4	10	13*	7

N Alternative
     Compromise
     (50 units)
	2.5	2.5	10	10	10

S Alternative 1 Buy the land 2 Lots of land 3 Coop. action 4 Retraining	4.5	4.5	18	18**	18**

* = this is the highest total in the column before considering the SOS alternative.
** = this is the highest total in the column after considering the SOS alternative.

The two key goals in the controversy tend to be agricultural productivity and a more equalitarian or equitable distribution of land ownership. The conservative alternative (by allowing for economies of scale that are associated with large land holdings) is more productive, but less equitable. The liberal alternative (of widespread land distribution) is less productive, but more equitable. The neutral compromise is somewhere between those relation scores, just as it is somewhere between the conservative and liberal distribution alternatives.

With these relation scores, we logically have the result mentioned above, where the conservative alternative wins with the conservative weights and the liberal alternative wins with the liberal weights. We are also likely to get the classic compromise, which is everybody's second-best alternative or worse. The 'or worse' means that sometimes liberals accept the compromise when the conservative alternative actually does better on the liberal weights, or the conservatives accept the compromise when the liberal alternative actually does better on the conservative weights. Each side may accept the compromise even though it is the third-best alternative to them, because they do not want to give in to the other side. That is not the case with Table 6.6, but it does sometimes occur in the psychology of public policy making.

The Super-optimum Alternative

The super-optimum alternative seems to involve three key elements. The first is that the land needs to be brought from the present landowners, rather than confiscated. If the owners are threatened with confiscation, one possible reaction is (1) to establish death squads, (2) to bring in American military power, or (3) to do other especially nasty things that may easily cost more for the US and the landowners than the cost of buying the land. The United States probably could have saved a fortune in military and other expenditures on Nicaragua, El Salvador and Guatemala over the last 10 or 20 years by simply using a fraction of the money spent to buy land from the owners to give to the peasants. The landowners would also have probably saved money, some of their lives, and great distress by paying a substantial portion of the taxes needed to buy the land.

The second element is that lots of land needs to be involved. It cannot be a token program. The landless peasants in developing countries are no longer as passive as they once were. They cannot be easily bought off with trinkets, pie-in-the-sky religion, patronizing aristocrats and other relatively worthless bribes or distractions. They have demonstrated a willingness to fight and die for land in pre-communist China, in Central America and in other developing countries, including the Philippines.

The third element is the need to use modern technologies in a cooperative way to overcome the divisive effect of distributing the land in relatively small parcels to the landless peasants. Here is where the policy makers can learn from both capitalistic American farmers and communistic Russian farmers. American farmers are highly individualistic, but they recognize that it makes no sense for each of them to own their own grain elevators, combines and other big equipment which they can own collectively through producer cooperatives. In the Soviet Union, agricultural efficiency has been promoted through machine tractor stations where farmers can share collectively tractors which they cannot afford to own separately. This is true regardless of whether the individual farmers are associated with collective farms or private plots. Cooperative activities also involve the equivalent of county agents who help bring farmers together to learn about the latest seeds, herbicides, pesticides and fertilizers and to acquire other useful knowledge. Cooperative action can also include credit unions and drawing upon collective taxes for well-placed subsidies to encourage the diffusion of useful innovations.

The fourth element is to train the farmers for new non-farming jobs. This includes the former landless farmers who cannot be accommodated with land, or who would prefer to get out of farming. It also includes the newly landed farmers who themselves or whose children might be better off in non-farming jobs. Caesar Chavez was the beloved leader of the American Farmworkers Union, which especially meant landless Chicano grape pickers. He advocated retraining and other job-finding facilitators as a long-term or intermediate-run solution to landless peasantry, somewhat on the model of FDR's Rural Rehabilitation Administration. Chavez recognized that grape picking and other farm labor could soon be done more profitably by machines. Thus land redistribution may only be a temporary solution for most landless peasants.

The important point from the perspective of international and intranational dispute resolution is that the severe class conflict resulting from landless or impoverished peasantry can lead to both kinds of disputes. Central America is a good example of the USA and USSR choosing sides between the conflicting classes. Haiti, Cambodia and the Zapatistas in Mexico offer dramatic examples of internal killings over land ownership and the inability of small low-technology peasant plots to compete internationally. Related examples of urban guerrillas and death squads have been seen in such countries as Uruguay, Brazil and pre-Castro Cuba. The urban causes involve problems of labor, consumers and housing.

With the above combination of SOS elements, one can have agricultural productivity and equity simultaneously. Doing so enables that combination of elements to be a strong winner on both the liberal totals and the conservative totals. Appropriate timing may also be required in the sense of moving fast to implement these kinds of ideas. The longer the delay, the more difficult such as SOS solution becomes, the reason being that the liberal left may acquire such a negative attitude toward the conservative right that the liberal left would consider buying the land to be a surrender to evil people. Likewise, the conservative right may acquire such a negative attitude toward the peasant guerrillas that they can see no respectable solution other than extermination of what they consider to be terrorists.

The Pro-democracy Movement: The Uprising in Thailand

Causes

Long-term causes might include:
1. Industrialization causing education which causes resistance to being ordered about by a dictatorial government.
2. Historical events such as:
    a. 1932. Thailand ended absolute monarchy. Replaced by military-controlled government.
    b. 1973. Successful student revolt with much loss of life.

c. 1976. Restored military rule until 1988.
d. 1988. Civilian rule.
e. 1991. Military coup.

The immediate causes might include:
1. For the coup
   a. Choice of deputy defense minister.
   b. Choice of army commander-in-chief.
   c. Choice of investigator of assassination plot.
2. For the pro-democracy demonstration
   a. Recent election in March. First prime minister was in drugs.
   b. Promise of Suchinda not to be prime minister.
   c. Wipe out corruption, but appointed leading crooks.
   d. Refusal to call special election.
   e. Refusal to allow constitutional amendment with grandfather clause.
3. For the killings
   a. Virtually no use of water cannon, tear gas or rubber bullets; instead, automatic weapons, long clubs and few shields.
   b. Alleges students shoot first, communist takeover, disrupt the monarchy.
   c. Isolated head, given middle-class involvement, the provinces and some segments of the military.
   d. A cornered madman concerned about face.

Remedies

The immediate remedies might include:
1. Pressure from abroad
   a. Total embargo.
   b. Boycott all Thailand products.
   c. Like South Africa.
2. Pressure from within
   a. Business.
   b. University support for resignation.
   c. More demonstrations, not less.
   d. Military opposition.
   e. Provincial opposition.
   f. Middle-class professionals.
   g. Monarchy, including king, crown princess and crown prince.
   h. Mass media.

The long-term remedies might include:
1. Withdrawal of US support for the military
2. Legal changes
   a. Constitutional amendment that no prime minister, civil service or government position while still military.
   b. No prime minister who is not elected.
   c. No military use for crowd control, just police.
3. Socialization into democratic principles of freedom to disagree with government and to be allowed to convert others.

Predictions

Short-term predictions might include:
1. The military may refuse to step down. They may stall for time, thinking that will lead to loss of interest by demonstrators.
2. Demonstrators and opposition parties will become impatient and again take to the streets, this time possibly with more anger inspired by perceived support from many or even all major segments of Thai society, including some of the military.
3. A stubborn, vicious military like Suchinda, Kaset and Issaprong may order troops to stop angry demonstrators. Then killings on both sides could be worse then before.
4. The alternative is face-saving departure with big money to go overseas as in the past.

Long-term predictions might include:
1. Parties along conservative and liberal lines instead of personalized groups.
2. Maybe judicial enforcement of the constitution.
3. More international, more American, and thus more regard for free speech, due process and treatment on merit.
4. Contracting out as SOS between private and government ownership and operation.

Implications from the Thailand Crisis Case Study

With regard to the problem of civilian versus military government. The SOS is (a) to phase out military rule to establish civilian rule, (b) that no military person should be in a policy job while in the military, and (c) that only the police should be used for crowd control – not the army.

Resolution of the problem of stability versus modernization requires well-placed subsidies and tax breaks to bring quality modernization. That means upgrading the skills of workers, mainly through on-the-job training, including workers who are displaced by new technologies. It also means facilitating the adoption of new technologies that create jobs, improve productivity and increase exports. Emphasizing quality implies (a) workplace safety and quality (b) environmental quality, and (c) quality consumer products.

There is the causal analysis problem of explaining the success of the pro-democracy demonstrations in Thailand as contrasted to their failure in Tiananmen Square. A further problem concerns the inconsistencies on the part of American foreign policy that relate to interfering with foreign governments in the cold war or the drug war, but not even offering non-interfering assistance on behalf of pro-democracy forces.

The role of middle-class people in bringing about social change is a key factor that we have emphasized before as essential to the maintenance of a stable democracy. There is much greater respect for intellectual input in developing countries or, for that matter, in almost any countries than there is in the United States. There is high regard by people in Thailand for what people in the Thailand universities are advocating. The *Bangkok Post* headline said, 'Academics Demand a New Government'. Behind that is some of the explanation for why Japan is doing better than the United States in learning new technologies Japanese business people, like Thai business people, have a high regard for university professors, especially American university professors.

There is a kind of quaint aspect of the Thai crisis that might have some interest to the Serbian royal family. They should observe how the Thai king handled the situation, which is nicely covered in the May 1992 headline in the *Bangkok Post*, that the King tells the factions to work on compromise. Immediately that was the end of the whole violence, demonstrations, and everything immediately reverted to a peaceful state. This is not because the Thai people are monarchists; it is because the Thai royal family knows how to be respected. The Thai royal family is to a considerable extent responsible for the high regard for higher education. Every higher education degree is personally handed to the recipient by a member of the royal family at graduation time. The family has a family tree filled with PhDs and MDs, with the son who is probably next in line for the throne also having a PhD degree.

The role of legalistic action is also important in the Thai example, in that there is a strong consensus that the situation at its height could be defused through a constitutional amendment, and even now the constitutional amendment idea is important. In other countries, like Latin America, amending the constitution would be considered close to a farce, with not much enforcement. In Thailand, they take seriously what the constitution provides and want it to specify that no one can be prime minister unless the person is an elected member of Parliament, regardless of how many or what percentage of Parliament chooses a non-elected member to be prime minister.

The situation also illustrates how being stubborn and non-functional with regard to face saving can be self-destructive and interfere with an SOS. The military prime minister could easily have arranged for a special election to get elected. He would thereby remove the key objection, but he refused to do so on the grounds that that would be an admission of wrongdoing. Instead, he lost the job of prime minister. Even if he did not lose his life, he is in disgrace.

There are other implications from this case study which we need to write up. One is the importance of economic boycotts by the United States in bringing about favorable governmental changes. That occurred already in South Africa but not yet in China. A big factor that turned the business community against the military prime minister was the boycott that was already in effect, with numerous American importers canceling orders – not because they were so sympathetic to the pro-democracy movement (though that may have been part of it), but because they explicitly said or implied that they did not want to deal with some kind of 'banana republic' military dictatorship. They wanted responsible, businesslike people. The important thing is that that kind of economic pressure can definitely change government decision making. It is ridiculous for the Bush administration to say it would have no effect in China, South America or elsewhere. It simply reflects the fact that the Bush administration does not place a very high priority on changing overseas government decisions in a more pro-democracy direction and that selling a few more widgets is more important.

The case study also has international implications by virtue of setting an important precedent and role model for other developing nations that military dictatorships are not the solution to a country's problems. Thailand is highly regarded in the developing world. It is a newly industrialized country. Other newly industrialized countries are also getting rid of their military or civilian dictators, or lessening their power such as South Korea and Taiwan.

An especially exciting outcome of the Thailand crisis case study is that it generated the concept of an International Dispute Resolution (IDR) workshop. Such a workshop builds on the concept of an SOS workshop which the Policy Studies Organization has been conducting since its China workshops of 1989, 1991 and 1992. An SOS workshop is a gathering of professors, practitioners, graduate students and others to learn about methods for arriving at super-optimum solutions to public policy problems. Such solutions can enable conservatives, liberals and holders of other major viewpoints to all come out ahead of their best initial expectations simultaneously. An IDR workshop involves the same subject matter as an SOS workshop. It differs from the usual SOS workshop in that at least some of the participants are invited to attend because they are associated with nations, provinces, ethnic groups or other groups that are in violent conflict with each other. The workshops can last from a full day (or less) to a week (or longer). The idea is that, during that time, the people whose groups are normally in conflict will be stimulated to think more about how all sides or viewpoints can come out ahead of their best initial expectations simultaneously.

The IDR workshop that was conducted at Chulalongkorn University during the Thailand crisis was not premeditated. It was supposed to be an SOS workshop. It turned into an IDR workshop because, during the conducting of the SOS workshop, the Thailand crisis occurred. Partly by coincidence, the participants in the Thailand SOS–IDR workshop included such people as a colonel in the Bangkok police force and a pro-democracy former communist guerrilla teaching in the Public Administration Department. Some of the emotional interaction was defused by virtue of face-to-face contact. Some of it was also defused by virtue of the nature of the subject matter that was being discussed: how all sides in highly emotional disputes can come out ahead of their best initial expectations simultaneously. The Thailand crisis was resolved before anybody participating in the IDR–SOS workshop had an opportunity to communicate any of the ideas to their colleagues in the police system or among the demonstrators. Future IDR–SOS workshops are, however, now being planned that will include people simultaneously from India and Pakistan, and a separate workshop will include people simultaneously from mainland China and Taiwan.

Differences and Similarities between China and Thailand

Beijing had a 90-year-old dictator that people were waiting to die. This caused a restraint on pro-democracy demonstrations. Thailand had a 55-year-old military dictator who was in very good health. Nobody suggested waiting for him to die. Many people suggested ways to accelerate his death.

Beijing was actually more restrained in some ways than Thailand. It is a civilian dictatorship, not a military dictatorship. Civilian police, including unarmed police officers with clubs and some tear gas, were largely used to deal with the students. They could not use water cannon because Beijing does not have a water system that can get up enough pressure to do any blasting of people with water. The Thailand crowd control consisted of heavy-booted paratroopers with assault weapons including high-powered machine guns and tanks.

Thailand sought to exercise some constraint out of sensitivity to world opinion and the export–import business, and Beijing has also been sensitive to this. The cold war has now ended, and many parts of the world, including eastern Europe, Africa, Asia and Latin America, have taken great strides toward democratization. Thus world opinion and student opinion are less tolerant of dictatorships. The main thing that needs explaining is why the pro-democracy demonstrators succeeded in Thailand and failed in Beijing. The timing may be more important than the place. The Thai students failed in 1976 in the same place because the world has not ready for democracy as it is now including Thailand.

Another important difference between Thailand in 1992 and China in 1989 is that Thailand had opposition political parties. Those parties used the demonstrations to embarrass the government through the only partially controlled media. The Chinese government, on the other hand, has been able to more successfully repress opposition political parties and media than the less dictatorial Thai government.

Thailand also has a king who is favorable toward constitutional democracy. China, on the other hand, had a paramount leader who admired the dictatorship of Singapore. China also had a history of autocratic emperors followed by strong individuals like Sun Yat-Sen, Chiang Kai-shek, Mao Zedong, and Deng Xiaoping.

Examples of the World Moving Toward Greater Democracy

In eastern Europe around 1989, at the time of Tiananmen Square, virtually every country had a one-party communist dictatorship. They now have multi-party systems with more choices for the voters than can be found in the United States.

In Africa every founding father is either out or in big trouble. That includes Kwanda in Zambia (who was voted out); Mbuto in Zaire (who was forced out), and Moy in Kenya (who is trying to repress demonstrations). Nigeria, which is run by a military junta, is also in trouble. None of the democracies in Africa is in any trouble. The people in Africa are becoming increasingly educated and unwilling to be told what to do by military or non-military dictators.

The military dictators have been thrown out of Argentina, Chile, Brazil, Uruguay, Paraguay, Panama and Nicaragua. The only possible exception is Peru, and even Peru represents a move toward greater democracy in that the last presidential election resulted perhaps for the first time since the Incas, in somebody who was not part of the Spanish elite being elected. In this case it was somebody who was not even Hispanic but was Japanese.

In the fourth continent, Asia, progress is not enjoying the same success, although Thailand is an example of progress in that the military has been thrown out and the country is likely to have a civilian government on into the future. In Burma, the military has taken over more explicitly than in the past. Japan represents a one-party state as much as ever and sets a bad example. There are rumblings of democracy in Saudi Arabia and Kuwait, although movement is very slow. The Philippines have just completed a reasonably democratic election which is a big improvement on the previous Marcos non-elections. Taiwan has become more democratic. Mainland China has also become more democratic than it was under Mao and the Cultural Revolution. The Tiananmen Square incident was partly a manifestation of pro-democracy desires, even though they were not fulfilled.

What all this adds up to is that the world as a whole is becoming better educated as a result of industrialization and less willing to accept medieval or military dictatorships.

7 Exporting Democratic Rights as a Product

The object here is not to defend the Bill of Rights. The object is to argue that it is in the best interests of the United States to encourage other countries to adopt the Bill of Rights. Conservatives like George Bush would never take the position that they are opposed to free speech; they just take the position that what is good for the USA may not be so good for Saudi Arabia. They may say such things as that these are people who only recently abolished slavery and that you cannot expect them to move in just a couple of years from where the USA was in 1860 to where the USA is in 1990.

One good argument against this kind of nonsense is that Saudi Arabians in about the 1950s had never seen a cellular phone, but they did not have to pass through the Stone Age and all those that followed before they could buy a cellular phone from Motorola or AT&T. Motorola was glad to sell them one right away. One does not have to reinvent the Bill of Rights if it has already been invented; one can just buy it from whomever is selling it. As it happens, it is a free good that is available at no direct monetary cost.

Pro-US Arguments

By supporting a feudalistic monarchy, all we are getting is some very short-run bootlicking. The monarchy has no lasting power. It will soon be replaced by young, educated people. The monarchy, just like communist dictatorships, is providing education; it is not deliberately trying to keep people illiterate. If they are educated, they read about the Bill of Rights. They read about what goes on in other countries and in no time at all they want to change things. If we really want to keep the monarchy in power, we should advocate massive book burning. This should include the Koran, since it has a few subversive things to say about democracy. The feudalistic monarchy of Saudi Arabia would not tolerate burning the Koran. By being unwilling to burn the Koran, though, they are in effect undermining themselves. The Koran is one of the most equalitarian religious books.

By supporting free speech we can gain psychological benefits by feeling proud of ourselves instead of ashamed. People in the State Department, people who are tourists, people in universities do not have to apologize all the time for American foreign policy which runs so contrary to American ideals. By supporting free speech we facilitate the development of new ideas for improving other societies, which means making them more productive. This, in the intermediate run, without even having to wait for the long run, means they are likely to become better customers for the United States and better sellers to the United States. We do not make much money off feudalistic monarchies, as contrasted with dealing with Japan, which buys goods and, especially, which sells low-priced, high-quality goods that add to our standard of living. The Japanese never would have become as productive as they are if they had not had open debate on how they should go about doing so.

Supporting free speech in places like Saudi Arabia provides for safety valves that allow people to release steam and bring about social change through peaceful means. Otherwise, they take to guerrilla fighting, as in Central America. The USA in recent years has almost inevitably sided with the landlords, the feudalistic monarchies, the business people, against the guerrilla fighters who tend to be workers and peasants. As a result, the country is drawn into a war like Vietnam or what could have been another Vietnam in Central America. A key reason for the Persian Gulf war not being a Vietnam was that it was not workers and peasants against landlords, but one country trying to take over another.

Countries that lack free speech and so bottle up discontent tend to try to take the minds of their people off their problems by engaging in aggressive behavior toward other countries. This could partly explain Iraq's behavior toward Kuwait. The USA was drawn into a war due to the aggression that results from free speech not having been facilitated in the aggressor state. We certainly did not encourage dissent in Iraq so long as Saddam Hussein was doing our bidding in the war with Iran; nor was he giving Israel any trouble.

One could argue in favor of exporting free speech on altruistic grounds, in that it is good for other people just as it is good for us. That means bringing in all the arguments for free speech being good for people. We are not so interested in doing that here; here we are trying to argue that we are exporting free speech for selfish reasons meaning that it will help America's power in the world. We are arguing here in favor of exporting free speech basically because it is good for the quality of life in the USA, regardless of what it does for the other people.

Exporting Democratic Rights Compared to Exporting Other US Products

On exporting technologically innovative products there is no disagreement. The Bush administration would not say Saudi Arabia is not ready for our automobiles or our computers. The problem here is how to sell them IBM computers when they can buy Japanese computers or, for that matter, computers from Korea, Singapore or Taiwan that are just as good, or better, for less money.

Exporting technologically innovative products is different from exporting the Bill of Rights. There is no competition when it comes to exporting the Bill of Rights. No other country in the world can touch the United States with regard to what the US Supreme Court has done over the last 50 years regarding free speech, due process and equal treatment, partly with the help of Congress, administrative agencies, interest groups, and state and local governments. In the case of technologically innovative products, though, there is vigorous competition in the form of Japan, West Germany and numerous other countries. The problem here is more one of talking about well-placed subsidies and tax breaks, involving the business of incentives, competition, risk and positive thinking. All these ideas are much more oriented toward the technologically innovative, productive side than the Bill of Rights side of exporting.

Case Studies of Bad Exporting

There is no need to concentrate too much on Saudi Arabia, though that country is a good example. The USA has had Bill of Rights problems with every developing region of the world. As regards Asia, we could mention the Vietnam War, which ran so contrary to the US's democratic principles. We could mention losing mainland China to communism and losing Taiwan at least temporarily to a right wing dictator. We could mention the recent problems with the Philippines. All of which can be attributed to the USA failing to live up to its own principles expressed in the Bill of Rights. As for Latin America, we could mention every Central American people, and the dictatorships the USA encouraged in Chile, Argentina and Brazil.

In Europe, some of the blame for eastern Europe going communist is definitely attributable to the United States' failure to support democratic alternatives. Greece is a good example, with the anti-fascist guerrillas wanting to have a democratic society after the end of World War II and to throw out their monarchy. The Truman Plan came to the aid of the worst military junta, or one of the worst, that the world has ever known. The same thing happened with Turkey. That really in a way was inconsistent, since Truman did support the democratic socialists in France and Italy. He and the conservatives would say that there were not enough democratic socialists to support, and likewise in China or in Vietnam: that it was either support the fascists or support the communists, and the USA chose the fascists. That was untrue, though: all these places had enough of a core of democratic socialists to justify American support. Important conditions should have been attached to the support that was given to Chiang Kai-Shek, the Greek junta and the Turkish junta.

In Africa, the USA supported South Africa to the very end. In fact, some American conservatives have not yet caught up with the idea that the South African right wing is now participating in the dismantling of apartheid. Some American conservatives have such a kneejerk reaction for supporting reactionaries that, even when the reactionaries change position, the American conservatives fail to show flexibility. This is illustrated by the attacks that many American conservatives made on Nelson Mandela. For example, when he visited Florida, they called him a communist dupe partly because he thanked Fidel Castro for the support that Castro gave to the anti-apartheid cause. The USA has supported some of the most murderous killers in Mozambique and Angola, who were not ideological fascists but just roving murderous bandits, but as long as they say they are anti-communist they receive American arms, or at least they did when the cold war was in a hotter state.

So much for the southern part of Africa. With regard to the northern part, to the very end the USA sided with the colonialists in Algeria, Tunisia and Morocco, just as it did in Vietnam. The French did not cause the USA to be part of the Algerian War, largely because just like the government of South Africa, they decided to be flexible. The pro-American government in Vietnam, on the contrary, never showed any flexibility. If France had continued the Algerian War, the United States might eventually have been drawn in. In the case of the British colonies in Africa, Britain gave all of them up without much bloodshed. The same happened in India and Asia. (The bloodshed in India was mainly between Moslems and Hindus rather than between Britain and India.)

Case Studies of Good Exporting

We should give some examples of occasions where the United States has done some good and where it has paid off well with regard to exporting the Bill of Rights. The best example would be the Marshall Plan, with its political rather than its economic aspects in converting France and Italy into democracies when they were both run by fascists and before the USA intervened, but we perhaps have to go back over 100 years to find any other decent examples. They would include the Monroe Doctrine cases where the French were ousted from Mexico and the Spaniards from Cuba. The USA supported Simon Bolivar in throwing off Spanish colonial domination in the early 1800s. That may be the sum total of America's record in supporting anti-colonialism, but the above examples are good ones because they show that at least in those instances it was recognized that promoting the Bill of Rights could be in the best interests of the United States. Emperor Maximillian in Mexico was quickly got rid of during the civil war. The USA had good motives in getting rid of the Spanish from Cuba in the Spanish–American War, but made a mess of it in the Philippines by becoming the colonial power there after getting rid of Spain.

Some presidents have supported democratic forces and have been admired by people in developing nations for doing so. They include Carter, Kennedy and Roosevelt, all three of whom were thought to be sincere, especially regarding Latin America, but also with regard to the world in general. FDR was firmly opposed to Nazi and fascist dictatorships in Europe and Asia. Both Kennedy and Carter, though they never did much, were personally opposed to Franco in Spain and Salazar in Portugal. They did nothing to change those governments, but at least they did not invite them into a North Atlantic Treaty Organization or the European Economic Community – although France and England would not have had Spain or Portugal. Under Reagan or Bush, however, there might have been pressure placed on France and England to admit them on the grounds that they represent potential customers, regardless of their ideology.

The handling of eastern Europe as of the 1990s has not been so bad. That can be partly explained by saying that the democratic forces happen also to be in favor of a combination of free speech and free enterprise, glasnost and perestroika. If they were only in favor of free speech, they might not get much American support. China is a good example of a case where American support is available to a country that is in favor of free enterprise but not free speech. The Soviet situation is currently unclear as to what the State Department's position is and whether it is desirable in terms of a Bill of Rights position. Gorbachev is the inventor of glasnost and perestroika, but is being pushed out by more vigorous forces who may be operating too much in terms of a kind of naïveté as to how far Russia can be pushed currently and also too much in terms of personalities.

Yeltsin says things that sound more liberal, but he lacks the ability to pull them off. This is because he has so antagonized conservatives and the military in the Soviet Union, whereas Gorbachev is capable of appealing to both the left and the right and can be much more successful in bringing about political reforms. In that sense, Yeltsin played a kind of extreme anti-communist role in order to push Gorbachev further toward reform and to make him more acceptable to the conservatives. Sometimes it looked like Yeltsin was not just trying to push Gorbachev but was really trying to replace him. That did eventually happen.

The US continued to be supportive of Gorbachev, until he no longer had major support from the Russian people. He antagonized the communists by promoting capitalism (perestroika) and free speech (glasnost). He antagonized the conservatives and the liberal democrats by retaining his membership in the Communist Party.

As of 1997, the United States (meaning President Clinton and Secretary of State Albright) are highly supportive of President Yeltsin, not because he is a liberal democrat. Rather, the support is more pragmatically based on the reality that Russia has developed at least temporarily a three-party system with communists on the left, extreme nationalists on the right and Yeltsin and his people in the middle. Some day the Yeltsin group may become the equivalent of the American Republican Party or the British Conservative Party. The people who are likely to become the equivalent of the American Democratic Party or the British Labour Party are still rather disorganized. Gorbachev thinks along those lines, but he is too unpopular, as mentioned above.

Humanitarian versus National Interest Criteria in Making Foreign Policy Decisions

People differ on foreign policy. It is not that liberals are in favor of a kind of soft foreign policy or are pacifist or humanitarian, while the conservatives are in favor of a hard, tough foreign policy. That is absolute myth. It all depends on who the enemy is. It is amazing how soft and lovable conservatives can be when the enemy is Nazi Germany in the 1930s, but how tough they can be when the enemy is Communist Russia in the 1960s or 1970s.

Nor should the distinction between national interest and humanitarian criteria be considered the same as that between hard-line and pacifist. One can advocate a humanitarian approach for highly mercenary, hard-nosed reasons. The material in the SOS policy book does that partly, saying that humanitarian foreign policy is good business. We do much better business with democratic governments than with dictatorial ones. We can defend encouraging democracy on do-gooder grounds, but that is normally not very effective. If it can be defended on money-in-the-pocket grounds, it gets more support, as long as the defense is not made too crass.

Also, from a purely military perspective, promoting democracy is good. We have better allies among democratic countries than among dictatorial countries. France and England are more likely to be allies of the United States in any world conflict than whatever dictatorships are left in the world, or past ones like Franco's Spain. By definition, nationalistic dictators are not very cooperative. One thing that keeps fascists from taking over the world is that they are so nationalistic that they cannot work well with each other, whereas democracies can.

If we talk about the issue as being national interest versus humanitarian interest, we really have a tradeoff:

1 the national interest people sound like some kind of hard-hearted group that wants to be friends with any dictator that is pro-American;
2 the humanitarian interest people sound like a bunch of softies that maybe want to go to war on behalf of anybody that claims to be in favor of democracy, although the usual humanitarian types just endorse democratic governments but are not willing to fight for them. They still come out as being naïve regardless of whether they are pacifists or aggressive humanitarians.

When the issue is stated in these terms, it is hard to find a compromise. The national interest people sound like they are giving up the national interest, and the humanitarian people sound like they are being inhumane. One way to decrease the possibility of a compromise or an SOS solution is to label one side Total Righteousness I and the other side Total Righteousness II.

The point made here is not so much that talking in terms of national interest versus humanitarian interest leads to an inherent tradeoff conflict. The people who claim to be advocating the national interest are usually advocating their own ideological interest, in the sense that both liberals and conservatives tend to take a hard-line, hawkish position, depending on who the external enemy is. Likewise, the so-called humanitarians are highly flexible, depending on who the external enemy is. Conservatives show great humanitarian concern for what is going to happen to blacks in South Africa if there is a boycott. They do not, however, show such interest about blacks in the United States.

Different distinctions include the following:

1 truly hawkish people and truly pacifist people that are hawkish and pacifist no matter who the enemy is;
2 hawks and pacifists that flip-flop depending on who the enemy is;
3 those who advocate a national interest who support dictators, and those who advocate a national interest who support democratic governments;
4 pacifists who support democratic governments but not dictators, although they will support either democratic socialistic or democratic

capitalistic governments: in other words, in determining where the flip-flops occur, one may need to think in terms of capitalism versus socialism and democracy versus dictatorship.

A super-pacifist will support not going to war against Hitler. Likewise, a super-hawk would support going to war against Canada if Canada says something nasty, regardless of what effect going to war has on America's economic interest or whether the other country is capitalistic or socialistic, or dictatorial or democratic. The super-hawk overreacts to insults regardless of where they come from. The usual hawk overreacts to insults if they come from, say, a communist government, but it is all right for the pro-American Turkish government to torture American prisoners as long as they stay pro-American with regard to allowing American airbases on Turkish soil. That is one reason for the cold war hawks not liking Amnesty International, because AI finds fault with pro-American governments sometimes, and even with the United States government.

This section is not meant to be a taxonomy of hawks and doves or national interest people versus humanitarian people. It is meant to talk about how supporting democracy in dispute resolution and foreign policy is an SOS; it simultaneously promotes the national interest and humanitarian considerations.

One can put this into a broader historical perspective beginning with the 1900s. At that time the US was dominated by supporters of President McKinley who thought of foreign policy in terms of selfish imperialism and colonialism, as indicated by the conquest of the Philippines, Puerto Rico and Cuba and the gunboat diplomacy in Central America. The countervailing position was best indicated by Woodrow Wilson's idealism, especially toward (1) developing the League of Nations; (2) making the world safe for democracy; and (3) allowing for national self-determination.

During the 1920s, the prevailing attitude became isolationism, as indicated by the rejection of the League of Nations and the passage of the anti–free trade Smoot–Hawley Tariff. Then came Franklin Roosevelt's return to idealism and democratic evangelism, as manifested in (1) his Good Neighbor policy; (2) the US as an arsenal for democracy; and (3) support for the United Nations.

After FDR, the bipartisan cold war set in with the Truman Doctrine, Nixon's anti-communism, the Kennedy–Johnson Vietnam War, and the Reagan Evil Empire. Then we move into the present bipartisan win–win orientation, where both Bush and Clinton are supportive of free trade, which enables everybody to come out ahead.

On the matter of promoting democracy though, there are still (1) conservatives who say business and trade must come first and (2) liberals who are willing to lose business rather than lose their principles. The key point of this section though, is that pushing democracy can create societies among developing nations that are able to be or become better customers, sources of supply, and investment outlets for the US and everybody.[1]

Note

1. Also see Chapter 11 below on 'USIA Win–Win Traveling Seminars', especially the section on 'Win–Win US Foreign Policy'. That section emphasizes promoting democracy, as well as peace and prosperity.

8 Mini-symposium on International Prosperity

The best international policies are those that promote international peace, democracy and prosperity. In the Autumn 1996 issue of the *Developmental Policy Studies Newsletter–Journal*, there was a mini-symposium on 'Inter- and Intra-National Dispute Resolution' dealing with peace issues. The Winter issue of the same year also contained a relevant item on 'The U.S. and the U.N'. The Autumn 1996 issue of the *Developmental Policy Studies Newsletter* dealt with 'Exporting the Bill of Rights', and the Winter issue with 'Human Rights and Developing Countries'. These articles considered democracy issues. Also see Chapters 7 and 14 of this book. The present Spring 1997 issue has a mini-symposium on 'International Prosperity'; it deals with issues that relate to the exchange of goods, people, factories and ideas, as well as general exchange facilitators.

The three goals of international peace, democracy and prosperity are pulled together in the Summer 1996 issue: under (1) 'Economic Policy' and 'Technology Policy' to promote prosperity, (2) 'Political Policy' to promote democracy and (3) 'Social Policy' to promote peace in the context of ethnic friction. The Winter 1996 issue also seeks to integrate peace, prosperity and democracy in US foreign policy in an article on 'USIA Win–Win Traveling Seminars'. Also see Chapter 11 of this book and Chapters 7, 8 and 10 of Nagel, *Developmental Policy Studies* (Ashgate, 1998).

Exchange of Goods

Improving International Competitiveness (Table 8.1, Row 1)

The conservative position (as indicated under the Bush administration) has been to emphasize that government regulation increases business expenses and thereby reduces international competitiveness. The liberal position (as

Table 8.1 Exchange of goods

Issues	Conservative	Liberal	Neutral	Super-optimum solutions
1 International competitiveness	1 Business profits	1 Labor and consumers	1 International competitiveness	1 Government investment in technology diffusion and upgrading of skills
	1 Decrease government regulation	1 Lower tariffs 2 Anti-trust action 3 Labor–management teamwork	1 Keep as is	
2 Tariff height	1 High profits	1 High wages	1 Low prices 2 Low taxes	1 Well-placed subsidies and tax breaks
	1 Pro-business conservatives, high tariffs 2 Free world market conservatives, low tariffs	1 Pro-union liberals, high tariffs 2 Internationalist liberals, low tariffs	1 Middling tariffs	
3 Getting reduced tariffs	1 Reducing foreign tariffs 2 Conservative perception	1 Reducing foreign tariffs 2 Liberal perception		1 Subsidy to bypass foreign tariffs 2 Positive incentives
	1 Threaten retaliatory tariff increase	1 Negotiating mutual tariff reduction	1 Some of both	

Mini-symposium on International Prosperity   95

4 Negotiating food sales outlets	1 Aid US producers (raise profits) — 1 Retaliatory tariff increases (+20%)	1 Aid US consumers (lower prices) — 1 Lower US tariffs without return (−20%)	1 Keep tariffs as they are	1 Reciprocal tariff reduction
5 NAFTA	1 Non-competitive US firms and workers — 1 Opponents 2 Labor unions and weak business firms	1 US exporters and investors 2 US consumers — 1 Advocates 2 Intellectual liberals 3 Business interests	1 Middling	1 Free trade 2 Retraining 3 Side agreements 4 Expanding economy

Note: In columns 2–4, goals are given first and alternatives second.

indicated under the Carter administration) has been to emphasize the need to lower tariffs, break up monopolies and encourage more labor–management teamwork. The neutral position has been to avoid substantial changes in regulation, tariffs and other such controversies.

The SOS alternative (as indicated by some elements under the Clinton administration) is to emphasize government investment in technological diffusion and the upgrading of skills. This alternative is capable of increasing the profits of business and the wages of labor. It can also result in better products at lower prices for both domestic and international markets.

Evaluating Alternative Positions on Tariffs (Table 8.1, Row 2)

On the issue of tariffs, conservatives who believe in free competitive markets both internationally and domestically tend to favor low tariffs. So do liberals who have an internationalistic orientation and who recognize the mutual benefits from buying overseas goods that have low prices, high quality and the ability to stimulate competitive activity on the part of American firms. On the other hand, conservatives who support monopolistic American businesses with their unreasonable profits are in favor of high tariffs. Likewise, pro-union liberals who do not want foreign competition are also in favor of high tariffs.

Traditionally, American conservatives have supported high tariffs and American liberals have supported low tariffs. The new SOS position is to support low or no tariffs, especially to stimulate worldwide competition to the long-run benefit of more efficient production and more prosperous consumption. The object is to develop plans for well-placed subsidies and tax breaks that will enable the United States to compete effectively for world market shares without the interference and mutual downgrading of high tariffs. That especially means encouraging the adoption and diffusion of new technologies, and the upgrading of worker skills to be able to put the new technologies to good use. The result, at least in the long run, is likely to be high business profits, high workers' wages, low consumer prices, high consumer quality and lower tax rates in view of the increased GNP as a tax base.

Getting Japan and Other Countries to Reduce Tariffs (Table 8.1, Row 3)

On this policy problem, conservatives and liberals have the same general goal of reducing foreign tariffs. For there to be a controversy, there must be a difference of opinion as to the best alternative to use in achieving that goal. The conservative position tends to emphasize retaliatory raising of tariffs as the most effective way of reducing foreign tariffs. The liberal position tends to emphasize negotiation and bargaining without explicit threats, but with promises of mutual tariff reduction. The neutral position is some of both.

There is a controversy here because conservatives and liberals perceive differently the relations between the alternatives and their shared goal. The conservative perception is that threats will do well, but conciliatory negotiation will not do so well. The liberal perceive that negotiating is more likely to do well, and that threats will not do so well.

In calculating the total scores, conservatives give more weight to their perceptions than to the perceptions of liberals. Likewise, liberals give more weights to their perceptions. On a 1-3 scale, each group gives a weight or multiplier of about 3 to its own perceptions and a weight of about 1 to the other group's perceptions. The super-optimum solution should be perceived as doing better than the neutral alternative by both conservatives and liberals. That enables the SOS to score higher on the conservative totals than the conservative alternative, and higher on the liberal totals than the liberal alternative.

The SOS might include a subsidy to enable efficient domestic producers to bypass the foreign tariff. For example, if US rice producers are unable to sell to Japanese consumers because there is a $1 tariff on each bushel of rice, it might be worthwhile for the US government to subsidize the rice farmers to the extent of $0.90 per bushel. This might be enough to enable them to make a profit in spite of the Japanese tariff. It would be worth it to the US government if the subsidy keeps a lot of people employed and brings in a large amount of income to add to the GNP. Otherwise, the subsidy may not be cost-effective. Such a subsidy is more likely to make sense where the Japanese government is under intense pressure from a politically powerful Japanese industry to retain the tariff.

The SOS can also include positive incentives. An example might be that the USA will agree to share in developing or marketing a new technology with Japan in return for a lowering of the tariff on rice. That positive incentive may be enough to stimulate the Japanese government to find a different way to subsidize Japanese rice farmers, rather than providing them with a tariff which harms Japanese food consumption.

Negotiating Free Trade in Farm Products (Table 8.1, Row 4)

This part of the table is based on a September 1993 news report that the US was seeking to have France reduce its subsidies to French soybean farmers. A $1 subsidy can have the same effect as a $1 tariff. In the case of the $1 tariff, a $2 quantity of US soybeans costs the French consumer $3, which is higher than the $2.50 that the French farmer charges. In the case of the $1 subsidy, the French farmer can make a profit by charging $1.50, which undercuts the $2 charged by the American farmer.

The conservative US negotiator threatens a big tariff increase on French wines to force the soybean subsidy down. This may help American wine producers, but it harms American wine consumers. The liberal US negotiator may lower US wine tariffs without receiving much in return. This harms US wine producers, but it helps American wine consumers.

The SOS may be to agree to lower the US tariff on French wines if France will lower the subsidy on French soybeans. The result is that US soybean producers, US wine consumers and French soybean consumers are all helped. The reciprocal arrangement is a net plus to the USA if there are more soybean producers than wine producers, and if the US wine producers can be diverted into something more plausible. The arrangement is also a net plus to France if they have more wine producers than soybean producers, and the French soybean producers can be diverted into something more profitable.

This kind of mutually beneficial reciprocal tariff reduction is a good example of an SOS solution where all sides come out ahead. This can be contrasted to a neutral compromise between a retaliatory increase and a unilateral decrease. Such a compromise of retaining the tariffs may harm US soybean producers, US wine consumers, French wine producers and French soybean consumers. The harm is greater than a reciprocal reduction, although not so bad as a retaliatory tariff increase on French wines, which may even increase French farm subsidies, rather than reduce them.

The North American Free Trade Agreement (Table 8.1, Row 5)

US exporters and investors are helped by free trade with Mexico and other places because (1) Mexicans can buy more US products if there are no Mexican tariffs artificially raising the price of American products, (2) Mexicans can buy more US products if they have more income as a result of working in factories that have expanded because of American capital, and (3) US investors can make money and add to the US GNP by investing in Mexican factories which are now able to export better to the USA because US tariffs have been dropped.

US consumers are helped by free trade with Mexico and other places because (1) they can buy products made in Mexico at lower prices because they no longer have a US tariff artificially raising them, (2) they can benefit from low prices that should result from decreased labor expenses associated with some products made in Mexico, possibly stimulated by American capital, and (3) US consumers include business firms that buy producer goods less expensively from Mexico and thereby make American firms more internationally competitive.

US firms and workers who are not sufficiently competitive would be harmed by the NAFTA agreement, but this can be minimized by (1) retraining workers and firms so that they can be more competitive in their old products or new products, (2) side agreements with Mexico that require upgrading of labor standards in Mexico, and (3) the possibility of disrupted workers and firms benefiting from the increased prosperity of the USA as a result of more exporting, better overseas investing and better buys for US consumers.

Mexicans can benefit in the same ways as Americans by just substituting for the three goal-columns (1) Mexican exporters and investors, (2) non-competitive Mexican firms and workers, and (3) Mexican consumers.

The opponents of NAFTA are referred to in this table as conservatives, and the advocates are referred to as liberals. This is done partly to simplify the calculation of the tools. It is also in accordance with the fact that conservatives have traditionally been in favor of high tariffs, although that is less true of recent years than of the period from about 1800 to the 1930s.

Exchange of People

US Immigration Policy (Table 8.2, Row 1)

To say that conservatives favor more restrictions on immigration than liberals do is not quite true. Those who favor restrictions do tend to be people who emphasize racial purity, but also working people who resist immigrant competition. Likewise, those who favor relaxing restrictions may be liberals who want to provide opportunities to minority people from developing nations, but also conservative business people who welcome cheap labor.

Greatly restricting immigration could involve having very low quotas for different parts of the world. It could mean requiring jobs in advance or having relatives in the USA. Mildly restricting immigration means allowing much higher immigration figures and not requiring jobs in advance. Greatly restricting immigration does tend to avoid unemployment of American workers, at least in the short run. In the long run, ambitious immigrants may enhance the economy and so provide more employment opportunities. Mildly restricting immigration does welcome ambitious people, although it may also welcome people who could be a drain on the economy.

An SOS solution that enables all sides to come out ahead might emphasize jobs for displaced workers. That would mean special programs to upgrade the skills or workers in areas where there is high immigration. An SOS solution might also emphasize ambition criteria in determining who is

Table 8.2 Exchange of people

Issues	Conservative	Liberal	Neutral	Super-optimum solutions
1 Immigration	1 Avoid unemployment 1 Greatly restrict immigration	1 Welcome ambitious people 1 Mildly restrict immigration	1 In-between	1 Jobs for displaced workers and ambition criteria
2 Refugees	1 Protect national purity 1 Refugees out	1 Promote quality of life of refugees and society 1 Refugees in	1 In-between	1 Upgrade skills
3 Volunteerism	1 Cost saving and efficiency 1 Buy technical assistance	1 Effectiveness 1 Rely on do-gooders	1 Volunteerism agencies, e.g. Peace Corps	1 Work through professional associations

eligible to come to the USA. Such criteria might favor those who are seeking higher education themselves or educational opportunities for their children. Such criteria might exclude people who have a high probability of being on public aid, as indicated by various predictive characteristics, including responses to interviews. If an immigrant does commit a crime or wrongly applies for public aid, he can be sent back with both a free ticket and a suspended sentence to be reinstituted if he breaks the terms of the sentence.

International Refugees (Table 8.2, Row 2)

International refugees are people who have been forced out of their nations by war or natural disasters, and they are at least temporarily waiting to return, or to go on elsewhere. Emigrants are people who are voluntarily leaving their homes and going to other nations where they are considered immigrants.

The conservative position is to keep refugees out, partly to protect national purity, but also to avoid competition for jobs. The liberal position is to let refugees in, partly to help them, out of sympathy, but also in recognition that they may provide useful labor and innovative ideas themselves or through their children. The compromise is to let some refugees in, but on a selective basis with restrictions.

The SOS solution might be to upgrade the skills of international refugees through organized international efforts, possibly under the direction of the United Nations. With greater skills, the refugees might be more acceptable to both conservatives and liberals, given their increased productivity and ability to enhance the economies of the countries to which they go.

Volunteerism in Technical Assistance (Table 8.2, Row 3)

Hiring expensive, experienced technicians for technical assistance programs may be highly effective in producing results desired by liberals, but it is contrary to cost saving desired by conservatives. Relying on the initiative of idealistic volunteers like missionaries may not be so effective, but it is cost-saving. The neutral compromise is to have volunteers in the field, but salaried professionals in Washington government agencies like the Peace Corps.

Each major alternative can be referred to as Position 1 and Position 2, rather than as conservative or liberal. Position 1 (relying on volunteers) is conservative in having low cost, but not conservative in producing pro-business results. Position 2 (relying on paid professionals) is liberal or generous in spending, but not liberal in results in being pro-labor or pro-consumer.

The SOS alternative might be to work through professional associations. For example, engineering associations would actively recruit engineering volunteers; lawyer associations would recruit lawyer volunteers, and so on. One would thereby get highly-placed experts for the price of idealistic volunteers.

Exchange of Factories

Foreign Factories in the United States (Table 8.3, Row 1)

The basic issue here is whether encouraging foreign factories to locate in the United States provides more benefits than costs in terms of the national employment and income. The benefits mainly consist of providing jobs for Americans who work in the factories. The costs mainly consist of increasing the competitiveness of foreign firms to take away American customers from American firms and thereby decrease employment in those American firms.

Encouragement of foreign factories could consist of tax benefits and subsidies or simply being allowed in on an equal basis with American factories. The issue is similar to the issue of allowing foreign products into the United States on an equal basis with American products, meaning no tariffs or other restrictions. Doing so is good for the American consumer; it also stimulates American business to operate more efficiently and makes it easier for American firms to sell overseas.

In addition to the same consumer benefits of not having tariffs on foreign products, encouraging foreign factories provides American job opportunities. It does, however, increase foreign competitiveness by reducing transport costs. It may also make American consumers more willing to buy, knowing that the products have been made in the United States, even though the firm is headquartered elsewhere.

There is currently division within the Clinton administration on this issue, but those in favor of encouraging foreign factories are winning, on the grounds that there is a net increase in jobs and other benefits. The Clinton compromise may result in a net increase in jobs, but (at least in the short run) it also results in a decrease in the profits of competing American business firms. The net increase in jobs, though, may result in an overall increase in the GNP, more than offsetting the decrease in profits.

An SOS solution would seek to increase both US jobs and US profits if possible. Providing encouragement or at least equal access scores reasonably well on jobs. To have a policy that also scores reasonably well on profits, it would be helpful to have an organized program to help American business firms that are being subjected to increased competition by the

Mini-symposium on International Prosperity 103

Table 8.3 Exchange of factories

Issues	Conservative	Liberal	Neutral	Super-optimum solutions
1 Foreign factories in USA	1 US profits 1 No encouragement for foreign factories in USA	1 US jobs 1 Substantial encouragement	1 In between	1 Improve competitiveness of US firms
2 US factories abroad	1 Business profits 1 No constraints	1 Good working conditions 1 Prohibits US firms abroad from violating fair labor standards	1 No free trade agreements without fair labor guarantees	1 Free trade agreements with guarantees 2 Import tax on goods made with unfair labor standards

foreign factories locating in the USA. That does not mean aid in the form of a bail-out or hand-out. It means seed money or investment money to improve their technologies and upgrade the skills of their workers so that they can be truly more competitive with foreign factories both in the USA and overseas.

An SOS solution might also provide temporary investment money to enable American firms to build factories overseas to be closer to foreign markets. That may be a separate, although related, issue. Doing so provides jobs for foreign workers. There may still be a net gain to the US GNP if the foreign sales bring in US income that more than offsets the loss of jobs to foreign workers. This may be especially so if US factories overseas are supplemented by an expansion of related factories in the USA in order to supply those overseas factories with parts and related products.

US Factories Going Abroad (Table 8.3, Row 2)

The problem here is whether here should be any restrictions or encouragement relating to American companies locating factories abroad. The conservative position is no restrictions. The liberal position is to prohibit US firms from locating abroad where doing so involves going below American fair labor standards, as in the Fair Labor Standards Act, which covers minimum wages, maximum hours and child labor. A compromise position would be to allow companies to locate factories abroad with a relaxing of the FLSA standards, but still making them at least partly applicable.

Conservatives are interested in promoting business profits. Liberals are interested in promoting employment for American labor under good wages and working conditions. Business profits are promoted if an overseas factory has closer access to customers, raw materials or skilled inexpensive labor. Those profits become part of an increased US national income. Locating factories overseas can also facilitate selling abroad, which helps in the trade deficit whereby otherwise substantially more would be bought than would be sold. The US factories operating abroad may be producing products especially for the American market which can be sold at a lower price to Americans than if the products were made in factories located in the United States, where labor and resources might be more expensive.

The disruption to American employment can be reduced in various ways. One is to have free trade agreements with foreign countries whereby they agree to establish and enforce fair labor standards on American companies and other companies. Another approach is to subsidize the upgrading of relevant American labor skills to make American labor more competitive, or to enable displaced workers to go into other, higher-paying jobs. A third approach might be to place an import tax on goods made with unfair labor standards by US-owned companies or others. The companies could avoid the tax by upgrading their foreign labor standards.

This three-part package could be considered as moving in a super-optimum direction where both business and labor come out ahead. In the long run, the free movement of goods and factories across international boundaries would have the effect of raising the national income of all the countries involved, thereby producing a more general super-optimum solution.

The problem of US factories going abroad especially relates to factories moving to developing nations like Mexico or those of Southeast Asia. A partial justification is that doing so helps those developing nations to build up their economies so they can become better customers for American products, better suppliers to American producers and consumers, and better outlets for American investment. For example, wages earned by Mexican workers in US factories located in Mexico can be an important part of the ability of Mexico to buy American goods.

Exchange of Free Speech Ideas

Trade and Human Rights (Table 8.4, Row 1)

This analysis stems largely from the controversy over how far to go in withholding trade from China until human rights are given more recognition, but the problem applies to many countries that would like increased trade with the USA but lack a minimum level of domestic institutions.

The conservative position is to have trade without human rights conditions or prerequisites. The liberal position is to use trade to secure better human rights conditions, including the possibility of a pluralistic political system which allows two or more political parties that compete meaningfully for votes. A neutral position would think in terms of less substantial human rights, such as visits by Red Cross workers to political prisoners, but not ending political prisoners.

The conservative position is oriented toward American business profits. The liberal position is oriented toward spreading democracy. Each side endorses the other's goals, but not with equal weight.

The object of an SOS alternative would be to promote both trade and human rights, partly through education and communication. That means encouraging students from China and other such countries to come to the USA. Doing so means that they are more likely to return with American values such as democracy. It also means increasing the communication of democracy-related ideas by way of radio, television, newspapers, books and other means to China and other such countries.

Table 8.4 Exchange of free speech ideas

Issues	Conservative	Liberal	Neutral	Super-optimum solutions
1 Trade and human rights	1 Business profits	1 Spread democracy	—	1 Promoting trade and rights partly through education and communication
	1 Trade without human rights conditions	1 Trade with human rights conditions	1 Trade with slight conditions	
2 Copyright Piracy	1 Profits for copyright holders	1 Circulate literate	—	1 Government as an insurer
	1 Tariffs and sanctions for copyright piracy	1 No raising of tariffs for copyright piracy	1 Moderate raising	2 Mutual access to courts
				3 Payment of royalities

The SOS alternative also recognizes that trade, even without human rights conditions, can promote human rights by promoting prosperity and internal education. Democratic institutions can also promote prosperity and trade. There is thus reciprocal causation, even without the two being explicitly linked. When used to encourage human rights, trade needs to be presented more as a reward or bribe, than as a threat or punishment. Trade has worked well in encouraging democratic institutions in places like South Africa. It can backfire if it is withdrawn to the point where extremists come to power (as in Russia) or to the point where the economy suffers long-term destruction (as could happen in Haiti).

Trade can also be used as a bargaining chip for other purposes besides human rights conditions, such as tariff reduction and the opening of investment opportunities, which conservatives would endorse, too.

International Copyright Piracy (Table 8.4, Row 2)

The issue here is whether US tariffs should be raised in retaliation against copyright piracy by other countries. Such piracy means reprinting books and other materials contrary to the monopoly rights and possibly the royalty rights of the US copyright holders. The issue is not the use of trade sanctions to promote peace, tariff reductions or democracy on the part of other countries. These uses of trade sanctions seem more acceptable to liberals and conservatives, as contrasted to the use of trade sanctions to stop the free circulation of literature. Nor is the issue the use of trade sanctions to retaliate against patent piracy such as making clones of IBM computers without permission or royalties. That may be less of a problem because IBM and other manufacturers should be able to compete well by having efficiently low prices and high-quality products without needing a legal monopoly. They can also more easily sue large manufacturers, as contrasted to basement printing or VCR operations.

Those who advocate raising tariffs are seeking higher profits for copyright holders such as book publishers and movie companies. They argue that people will not write or publish books unless they can make big profits. However, the only books that are subject to copyright piracy tend to be books on which big profits are already being made. Those who advocate not raising tariffs are interested in seeing the circulation of American books, music, movies and related materials to the rest of the world. They tend to believe that such circulation generally promotes the kinds of values the USA endorses, including democracy, prosperity and peace.

An SOS solution that could enable both sides to come out ahead would be for the government to act as an insurer to copyright holders. The government would pay for part of their losses to copyright piracy in terms of the difference between the profits they are making and some reasonably high profit level. That profit level may be lower or higher than the profits they are currently making. Such a level might be expressed as a 100 per cent return on one's investment although possibly with a different level for different types of copyrights in terms of books, movies, music or software.

The SOS solution might also include mutual access to the courts of all countries to be able to bring lawsuits against pirating companies in order to collect reasonable royalties. Perhaps there could be an international court dealing with copyright, patents and trademarks. The problems are largely between private sector business firms rather than government manufacturing, but the governments could assume a responsibility for providing appropriate dispute resolution institutions and for paying non-prohibitive royalties.

General Exchange Facilitators

Dollar Exchange Rates (Table 8.5, Row 1)

A high dollar value means that one dollar will buy many units of the currencies of other countries. A low dollar value means that one dollar will buy relatively few units of the currencies of other countries. If the dollar has a relatively high value, the USA has difficulty selling to other countries because they have to give a lot of units of their currencies in order to get a dollar. If the dollar has relatively low value, the USA has difficulty buying from other countries because Americans have to give a lot of dollars in order to get the currencies of other countries.

If we concentrate on improving the quality and prices of American goods, we can sell a lot of American goods to other countries without lowering the value of the dollar. A big effect of selling a lot more to other countries is the increase in the American national income. That enables Americans to have a lot more money to buy from other countries without raising the value of the dollar.

Thus improving the quality and price of American goods through upgrading technologies and skills is a good SOS solution because it can achieve both goals of increased buying and increased selling simultaneously. This is in contrast to manipulating the dollar, which increases one goal but decreases the other in a typical tradeoff pattern.

International Economic Communities (Table 8.5, Row 2 and Table 6.5)

The relations between each alternative and each goal can be shown on a 1–5 relations scale in Table 6.5, where 5 means highly conducive to the goal, 4

Table 8.5 General exchange facilitators

Issues	Conservative	Liberal	Neutral	Super-optimum solutions
1 Dollar Exchange Rates	1 Buy from other countries — 1 High dollar value	1 Sell to other countries — 1 Low dollar value	 1 Middle dollar value	1 Improve quality and price of US goods
2 International Economic Communities	1 Preserve sovereignty and national strength 2 Satisfy national identity and emotions — 1 Nationalism and separatism	 1 Promote jobs and consumer goods — 1 One world	 — 1 Regional government	1 Economic community

Mini-symposium on International Prosperity   109

means mildly conducive, 3 means neither conducive nor adverse, 2 means mildly adverse and 1 means highly adverse to the goal.

The conservative goal is given a weight or multiplier of 3 by conservatives on a 1–3 scale of weights, but weight of 1 by liberals. The liberal goal is given a weight or multiplier of 1 by conservatives, but a weight of 3 by liberals.

A single asterisk can show the alternative that wins on the liberal totals before the SOS alternative is considered. It is likely to be the liberal alternative. A single asterisk can also show the alternative that wins on the conservative totals before considering the SOS alternative. It is likely to be the conservative alternative. A double asterisk can show the alternative or alternatives that win on each total after the SOS super-optimum solution is considered. The SOS should score higher than both the former conservative winner on the conservative totals, and simultaneously higher than the former liberal winner on the liberal totals.

Table 6.5 is then translated or simplified into the second row of Table 8.5 using only words instead of numbers.

The international economic community (IEC) scores well on the conservative goal of national identity and stature. No sovereignty is given up. Each member of the community gains some stature by being associated with a larger, more powerful body than itself. The IEC also promotes the liberal goal of quality in life in terms of jobs and consumer goods by (1) allowing for the free flow of job applicants across international boundaries, (2) removing tariff barriers to higher consumer standards of living, and (3) providing for a better division of labor among the countries, which facilitates more jobs and more consumer goods.

9 Global Policy Studies

What the Field Includes

The field of global policy studies can be defined as the study of international interactions designed to deal with shared public policy problems. Such policy problems may include the following:

1. trans-boundary problems such as people, pollution or goods literally going across international boundaries;
2. common property problems like those concerning the oceans, Antarctica or the atmosphere, which nobody owns but which are a kind of common good that needs to be regulated. Otherwise they will be devoured, to the mutual detriment of the nations of the world, like the loss of the commons meadows;
3. simultaneous problems, such as health, education and welfare, about which all countries can learn from each other.

How the Field Differs from Related Fields

Global policy studies is related to international relations, comparative government and public policy studies. None of those three political science fields, however, is currently studying adequately the subject of global policy studies. International relations concentrates on interactions among countries that relate to diplomacy, alliances and the resolution of disputes that might otherwise result in war. There are international institutions concerned with public policy studies, such as the specialized agencies of the United Nations, but they are not part of the mainstream of the study of international relations. One might also note that important international interactions associated with global policy studies, such as the economic summit meetings or other, even less formal meetings among government officials of various countries which are designed to deal with shared policy problems, may not be institutionalized.

The field of comparative public policy is cross-national in the sense of dealing with a multiplicity of countries. The analysis, however, tends to be of one country at a time. Sometimes comparisons are made across countries with an attempt to explain and evaluate differences and similarities, but the element of international interaction which is essential to global policy studies, is missing. 'Global' does not mean that all countries of the world interact simultaneously but rather that all countries of the world do share the policy problems under consideration, at least potentially.

The field of policy studies tends to concentrate on the single country of the political or social scientist who is working in the field. Some policy studies scholars do look to other countries, but mainly for the purpose of getting ideas that have predictive or prescriptive power within their own country. They seldom look to international interaction, although they may look at the interaction that occurs between states, provinces, cities or other subnational units within their country. If each country seeks to maximize its own quality of life without cooperative interaction, all countries may suffer important opportunity costs, as in other sub-optimizing situations. The classic example is that each country tries to produce whatever goods it produces best and, as a result, the world winds up with surpluses and shortages on all goods. It should, however, be noted that, in the absence of world government, it will be necessary for individual countries working together, by formal or informal agreement, to make use of the available positive and negative incentives for encouraging internationally desired behavior.

Multiple Dimensions

Global policy studies provides a good balance on a number of dimensions, including the theoretical, geographical, purpose or goal, disciplinary, ideological and methodological. There is a balance between cross-cutting theoretical matters and those that are more specific in nature. The theoretical orientation, however, is not overly abstract and the discussion of the specific policy problems does not emphasize anecdotal case studies. Balance among *various parts of the world* is represented by the researchers in the field, including political and social scientists from England, Germany, Poland, India, Spain, the Philippines and the United States. There is even better balance in terms of the countries that are referred to by the researchers, which include all major parts of the world.

Global policy studies provides balance between prescriptive, or evaluative, analysis and predictive, or explanatory, analysis. The field is thus concerned with both explaining variations in the occurrence of international interactions dealing with shared policy problems and prescribing how such international interactions can be improved to be more effective, efficient and equitable in achieving their goals.

With regard to balance across disciplinary perspectives, the researchers in the field are primarily political scientists, but they recognize that one cannot deal adequately with policy problems without bringing in the perspectives of other social sciences and other fields of knowledge such as economics, sociology, psychology and natural science. As for balance across ideological perspectives, the researchers in the field come from a variety of ideological backgrounds in terms of how government should relate to the economy or to the people and how government should be organized. There may, however, be an underlying pragmatism that is especially associated with policy studies as contrasted to political theory and a search for solutions to global policy problems that will be recognized as desirable, regardless of ideology. There may also be an underlying virtual unanimity in favor of an expansion of the elements of democracy that are conducive to academic creativity and interaction, as contrasted to balancing democracy and dictatorship.

Balance across methodological orientations includes studies that emphasize verbal or quantitative analysis. There may, however, be a tendency to get away from unstructured verbal description and make more use of systematic analytic frameworks such as multi-criteria decision making. Doing so involves analyzing a set of goals to be achieved, alternatives available for achieving them, and relations between goals and alternatives in order to choose or explain the best alternative, combination, allocation or predictive decision rule. There may also be a tendency to get away from unthinking cross-national quantitative description which involves correlating policy-irrelevant or -relevant variables against other variables or each other for 160 members of the United Nations.

Current Developments

It is difficult to say when the study of international interaction to deal with shared policy problems first began. One landmark book in the field is Marvin Soroos, *Beyond Sovereignty: The Challenge of Global Policy* (University of South Carolina Press, 1986). Before that, there were studies of specialized agencies within the United Nations and the League of Nations, including the International Labor Organization, the World Health Organization and other international agencies concerned with specific policy problems. That earlier literature tended to focus on those semi-governmental institutions rather than on more informal types of interaction. A key volume in the earlier literature is Robert Keohane and Joseph Nye, *Power and Interdependence: World Politics in Transition* (Little, Brown & Co., 1977).

An important event since the publication of the Soroos book is the development of the beginnings of a study group on 'Global Policy Studies' within the International Political Science Association (IPSA). A petition is now pending for the establishment of such a group. That petition arose as a result of the enthusiasm shown at the 1988 IPSA triannual meeting in Washington, DC at the global policy studies panels.

International Economic Communities

An exciting new development with regard to international interaction to deal with shared policy problems is the international economic community (IEC). This involves a group of countries agreeing to remove tariff barriers to the buying and selling of goods among them as a minimum agreement to constitute an IEC. The agreement may also provide for removal of immigration barriers to the free flow of labor, and a removal of whatever barriers might exist to the free flow of communication and ideas. The European Community is a good example, but other examples are developing in North America, Latin America, Africa, Asia and eastern Europe.

IECs can be viewed as super-optimum solutions where conservatives, liberals and other major viewpoint holders can all come out ahead of their best initial expectations simultaneously. The conservative alternative emphasizes nationalism and separatism. The liberal alternative emphasizes one world or world government. The neutral alternative emphasizes regional government, which involves political institutions more than an economic community.

The conservative goals emphasize national identity and stature. The liberal goals emphasize quality of life in terms of jobs and consumer goods. The conservative alternative does better on the conservative goals, as one would expect. The liberal alternative, however, does better on the liberal goal. Thus the traditional alternatives result in a tradeoff, where the overall winner depends on whether one has conservative goals or liberal goals.

The alternative of having an economic community does well on the conservative goal of preserving national identity since no sovereignty is lost in an IEC, as contrasted to the sovereignty that is lost in a world government or a regional government. The IEC may also add to the national stature of the component parts by giving them the increased strength that comes from being part of an important group. Thus France may have more national stature as a leader in the European Community than it has alone.

Likewise, the alternative of having an economic community does well on the liberal goal of promoting quality of life in terms of jobs and consumer goods. Jobs are facilitated by the increased exporting that the IEC countries are able to do. Jobs may also be facilitated by free movement of people to countries in the IEC that have a need for additional labor. Consumer goods are facilitated by the increased importing that the IEC countries are able to do without expensive tariffs.

PART III
TEACHING DEVELOPMENTAL POLICY STUDIES

10 Policy Analysis Training for Developmental Administrators

Vasant Moharir

Introduction

One of the main objectives of Working Group VII on Education and Training in Public Policy is to help member institutions, especially in developing countries with model curricula for short-term and long-term training and educational programs in public policy making. This is a task force group of the International Association of Schools and Institutes of Administration (IASIA). In the past the working group discussed these issues in a general way and at its last meeting, held in Brisbane in July 1988, special attention was paid to the problems of short-term training programs. For this I had prepared (in my role as project director) a special background paper and particular information about two such efforts in the Philippines and India were presented to the working group. On the basis of this the working group asked the project director to come up with general guidelines which would be of use to other member institutions which may be contemplating starting such training programs. The present chapter is a response to this. In preparing this chapter, the project director took into consideration whatever information was readily available to him, based on previous presentations to the working group and published literature on the subject. The suggested guidelines should, therefore, be taken as a general guidance, to be adjusted for the situation of each member institution. Also these guidelines may need revision after some time when more information about experience of other countries in this area is available.

Philosophy behind Short-term Training Programs

Contents, approach and teaching methods of any educational or training activity in the field of public policy are influenced by the conceptualization of the process of policy making and the role of administration therein. Without going into detailed arguments, it is stated at the outset that accumulated theoretical literature and actual experience of policy making in third world countries indicate that policy making needs to be conceptualized both as a problem-solving process and as a sociopolitical process. Technically oriented approaches assumes the policy-making process is merely a technical problem. The problem-solving process then stresses the narrow use of quantitative policy analysis techniques. (See Sue Richards, 'Training For Policy Management', paper presented to the European Institute of Public Administration, Round Table on Policy Analysis and Training of Public Servants, Maastricht, 22 July 1985.) On the other hand, viewing policy making merely as 'wheeling and dealing' and as a captive of interest group forces, is also misleading. Actual experience of the project director as a teacher of public policy in international programmes for civic servants from developing countries also makes him aware of the demand of many of his former students to be equipped with some analytical and problem-solving tools, in addition to a comprehensive understanding of the process of policy making.

Often research scholars, especially those from industrialized countries, think that rational analysis, based on facts and figures, does not constitute a major part of the decision-making process in developing countries and therefore devoting time to analytical techniques is a waste of time and may lead to disillusionment among graduates of such programs. While it is true that the prerequisites for an extensive use of complicated policy analysis techniques, such as availability of relevant data, presence of trained people who can make use of such techniques and a background of decision makers encouraging use of such techniques, may not be present in some of the developing countries, the scope for the use of rational techniques is grossly underestimated. There is one aspect of the decision-making scene from developing countries which may be quite positive here. There is already a tradition of using analysis as a basis for decision making in relation to developmental planning. Most developing countries have adopted a continuous process of economic and social development planning. This already involves use of many 'rational' techniques, such as input–output analysis, cost–benefit analysis and statistical analysis, and for the most part politicians accept the policy options arising out of such analyses. Even if the political leadership of many developing countries may not understand the principles of such analysis, they willingly accept conclusions arising out of it, partly because of pressure from external funding agencies and partly because of the desire to appear modern: to be seen using modern, rational techniques of analysis. So it is not that the leadership is averse to the use of analysis as a basis for policy making, but its use has to be seen within certain political parameters. As far as this factor is concerned, even in the industrialized countries political leaders have subordinated policy analysis units to overriding political considerations. Swings in the fortunes of the Central Policy Review Staff in England between the socialist and the conservative leadership demonstrates this (Sue Richards, 'Training For Policy Management'). In every country, industrialized or developing, there are certain 'holy cows' which policy analysis is not allowed to touch. But this does not exhaust the scope for policy analysis in many areas of public policy such as health, education and transport. Personal or party ideologies provide parameters within which analysis needs to be used, not abdicated. In view of this, the author is of the opinion that the approach to design and contents of short-term and long-term training and educational programs in public policy in developing countries should emphasize both short and long-term training. This is also supported by the limited available information about such courses in some of the developing countries.

In the final analysis, the philosophy of the training program will depend upon the specific objectives of training, laid down by the government leaders. In the third world context, the stated objectives of such training programs are often 'reformist', improving the ability of senior civil servants to formulate and implement public policies. The following statement of objectives of a training program organized by the College of Public Administration in the Philippines for the senior officials of the Department of Environment and Natural Resources is representative of the approach of similar institutions in other third world countries: 'to familiarize senior decision-makers of the Department with the basic concepts and principles of policy research and evaluation, as well as introduce them to the various tools and techniques of policy analysis' (G. Iglesias, *Training in Policy Analysis for Senior Decision Makers of DENR*, College of Public Administration, University of the Philippines, 1988).

Dror, who has developed and conducted intensive policy workshops for senior administrators in many countries, suggests that the objective of such short courses should be 'to increase the capacity of senior decision makers to handle complex policy issues and thus to augment their capacity to govern' (Y. Dror, 'Advanced Workshops in Policy Analysis for Senior Decision Makers: Lessons from Experience', in Stephen J. Wali and Sidney Mallick (eds), *The Practice of Management Development* (Praeger, 1988). In a paper entitled 'Civil servants, their education and the science of public administration in the Netherlands', submitted to the working group at its meeting in Milan in July 1987, Arthur Ringling suggested that the objective of such training should be 'both experience-supportive and experience-corrective'.

Even when we pay heed to the statement of Werner Jann that 'policy makers do not usually do analysis. They listen to arguments and judge them' ('Teaching Policy Analysis by the Case Method: Experiences and Lessons from the United States', paper presented to Round Table on Policy Analysis and Training of Public Servants, Maastricht, July 1985) public officials need to be trained as aggressive consumers or creative users of policy analysis and should understand the possibilities and limitations of various policy analysis methodologies. To this extent at least, the proposed approach should incorporate rational, analytical, problem-solving techniques. In other words, new short-term training programs in this area should aim at improving the understanding of senior administrators about the complexities of the policy-making process as well as equip them with the knowledge of some of the important analytical techniques.

Scope of Short-term Courses in Public Policy

The answer to the question, 'What should be the scope of short-term training programs in public policy?' depends upon the philosophy of such courses as well as their duration. Assuming the acceptance of the philosophy as indicated in the previous section, and assuming that the clientele of such courses would be very senior administrators (permanent secretaries, deputy permanent secretaries, directors arid director-generals of bureaus), it is desirable that the scope should cover policy formulation, implementation and evaluation, with more emphasis on policy formulation and police analysis. The experience of such training programs in India and the Philippines supports this. The above clientele is invariably involved as proximate advisers of ministers on important policy issues and their main responsibility is assisting in formulation of new policies or in reformulation of existing policies. In this connection inclusion of discussion on techniques for policy formulation such as cost–benefit analysis, scenario writing and multi-criteria analysis would be useful. Similarly, exposure to most common techniques of policy and program evaluation used in the third world context is desirable.

Only a limited amount of time can be devoted to discussion of policy implementation in such a short course. Most senior administrators do have substantive familiarity with the policy implementation process but only a few of them may appreciate the link between formulation and implementation and the need for more extensive analysis of 'implementation analysis' as part of analysis for policy formulation. Use of a suitable case, taking participants through all stages of policy making, can not only achieve the objective despite limitations of time, but can also help in showing the interlinkages between formulation, implementation and evaluation and viewing the policy cycle as a whole.

Structure of the Course

The detailed structure of the course is derived from the philosophy behind the training program and is scope. Both the literature and actual experience indicate the need to enmesh the worlds of theory and reality. Many authors have emphasized that policy analysis can be learnt only be doing analysis singly or in groups (see William A. Dunn, *Public Policy Analysis: An Introduction*, Prentice-Hall, 1981; Garry Brewer and Peter deLeon, *The Foundations of Policy Analysis*, Dorsey Press, 1983). This means that the structure of the course should provide for introduction to techniques and methods of policy analysis as well as 'hands-on' experience in doing policy analysis. Use of computer simulations for this purpose, as demonstrated to Working Group VII by Professor Stuart Nagel in Milan, in 1987, can serve a double purpose of 'removing the fear' of the computer and learning policy analysis in an active way.

Both the training program in India (Indian Institute of Public Administration, New Delhi, Administrative Staff College, Hyderabad) and the Philippines (College of Public Administration, Manila) reported at the working group meeting in Brisbane, had two well-defined parts. In the first part of the program, participants were exposed to various conceptual, theoretical aspects of policy making, including some of the policy analysis techniques, in the second part, participants examined in small groups particular current or past policy issues, with the help and guidance of the faculty.

Since in such programs certification is less important than improving insights, more group work rather than individual work is likely to be conducive to learning. Working on 'live policy issues would not only increase the motivation of the participants but would also enhance the relevance of the course. However, this requires considerable prior research and preparation by the course faculty, including discussion of political and other sensitivities which may be attached to such current policy issues.

If the period of the course is too short or the composition of the group too heterogeneous, individual policy analysis assignment may be desirable. Each course member may be required to choose a recent policy decision taken in his or her department and to present a report of, say, a thousand words to a new minister, showing why the decision was taken, who was concerned with it and what the effects have been (see Dennis L. Bird, 'Teaching Public Administration to British Civil Servants', VI, *Teaching Public Administration*, 1, 55–65 (Spring 1986).

Size and Composition of the Training Group

For effective learning and ease of communication between the participants and between participants and the faculty, the group should not be too large. Most of the existing training programs in third world countries are aiming at much bigger groups. The Philippine program aimed at a group of 30, with Hyderabad and New Delhi aiming at 25. Sometimes this is done at the planning stage, when a higher proportion of people who do not show up for the training sessions is assumed. From the point of view of group dynamics and effective learning, a group size of between 16 and 20 is desirable.

Should the training group for such a high-level training program/seminar be homogeneous in terms of level of civic servants and their functional area of experience, or should the group be mixed? The answer to this question depends upon a number of factors, including the culture of the civil service, the transferability of civil servants across functional and territorial areas and previous training received by civil servants.

Experience of existing programs indicates the usefulness of both approaches, mixed groups and homogeneous groups. When the need is for urgently improving policy performance in a particular policy area for political or other reasons, it may be desirable to have a homogeneous group from the same functional policy area. As part of the general program to improve policy analysis capabilities of civic servants throughout the civic service, mixed groups are to be preferred. If a training institute is initiating activities in this area, it is desirable that it gets some experience in organizing a few courses with a mixed clientele, emphasizing generic problems and issues of public policy. As indicated earlier, organizing training programs around a major live policy area requires considerable preparation on the part of the faculty.

Comparability of status and experience and more important considerations in the composition of the training group than age or sex. Limited experience of actual training programs indicates the need to emphasize certain minimum educational qualifications in order to derive maximum benefit. In the programs reviewed so far, this level was that of a bachelor's degree. Having in the training group participants with grass-roots experience of policy implementation would prove useful in realistic discussion of policy options. In this connection, it is interesting to examine whether a combined training group of political decision makers and senior administrators would not prove equally or more effective in sensitizing the politicians to rational analysis and civil servants to issues of political feasibility of policies. Although some stray examples of focused short-term seminars on particular issues with such a combined politicians–administrators groups have come to light, no regular activity on this basis is being reported in any country.

Duration of the Course

The actual duration of such a program depends upon the availability of senior civil servants for a long period of time and that of relevant teaching materials and qualified faculty. In view of the high-profile clientele of such programs, duration of longer than a couple of weeks is unrealistic. Most programs for this category in other subject areas do not exceed four or five working days. If part of the purpose in organizing such courses is to improve actual practice of policy making, one week is too short: it may be enough to create interest in policy analysis but not sufficient to provide sufficient exposure to some techniques and the opportunity for course members to try their hand at some live policy issues. Both in India and in the Philippines, a period of two to four weeks of rather intensive work has been found to be realistic, but this may not be feasible in other countries. At least the attempt should be made to have the group members for two weeks on a regular, continuous basis. Effectiveness can be much enhanced when participants stay together during the course. Organizing such a course on a part-time basis, spread over a period of time, needs to be avoided and should be used only as a last resort.

Contents of the Course

Contents of such programmes have to be decided according to the circumstances of each country and the length of time available. They also depend upon whether it is the policy part which needs to be emphasized or the management part, and whether the clientele is coming from one policy area or disparate policy areas.

Irrespective of the duration, the contents of every training program in this area should expose participants to both the analytical and sociopolitical dimensions of policy making and to significant issues of formulation, implementation and evaluation. If time is limited, a good case study can be used for this purpose. Content should include exposure to at least one or two techniques of policy analysis, such as cost–benefit analysis, multi-criteria analysis, scenario writing and political feasibility analysis. Inclusion of some examples of successful policies in the content would not only strengthen the belief that policies can be successful with better analysis but would also bring realism to the course.

In terms of suggestions for inclusion of specific subjects, the best one can do is to bring to the notice of member institutions curricula of a few existing programs from which topics could be selected according to circumstances. The final section of this chapter presents a summary of the contents of a one-week training program organized by Yehezkel Dror, a two-week program organized by the College of Public Administration, Manila, for a homogeneous training group, and a four-week program arranged by the Administrative Staff College, Hyderabad.

The World Bank has also been organizing such short-term courses in policy analysis at Washington and elsewhere. Most of these courses were on specific sectoral policy issues in which the World Bank had been involved, such as food supply, economic adjustment policies, reform of parastatals and energy policy (*World Bank Annual Report*, 1985, pp. 59–61). Although more details of the content of these programmes are not readily available, the approach seems to emphasize economic and financial analysis of policies, rather than policy analysis with a broader frame of reference.

The experience of other training institutions in Western Europe in this regard is not very helpful. Although the subject of policy studies and policy analysis was ranked number one in importance by a large number of senior civil servants from a sample of West European countries, as yet very few such courses have been launched on a regular basis (see Leo Klinkers and Lewis Gunn, 'Survey Among European Experts of Training and Education in Public Administration', Final Report, E.G.P.A., Brussels, No. 2/1984). The Institut International d'Administration Publique, in Paris, which organizes courses on various aspects of public administration for senior French civil servants and also for those from francophone third world countries, emphasizes governmental decision making during minor and major crises as part of the curriculum in public policy. The importance of including communication skills in training courses in policy studies has been stressed by another teacher of policy studies in England: Sheila Vaughan, 'Teaching Policy Presentation Skills – A Case Study', VII *Teaching Public Administration*, 2, 34–9 (Autumn 1987) and another trainer in an in-service training program in England has reported changing emphasis on management and efficiency considerations to the neglect of effectiveness and responsiveness in one-week regular training programs for middle-level civil servants (Sue Richards, 'Training For Policy Management').

Methods of Teaching

The need for non-conventional methods for teaching a subject like policy analysis has been stated by many scholars and trainers. Understanding and appreciating the complexities of policy making can be done much better through experiential learning than by being taught about it. The use of case studies, gaming and simulations is very useful in this context. The problem, however, in the context of the situation in developing countries, is the paucity of well written case studies on public policy, especially from the point of view of teaching.

In the courses at Hyderabad and Manila, mentioned earlier, a combination of the lecture method and its derivatives, such as lecture–discussion, lecture–exercises and practical group work, was used. Although practical examples from the national policy scene were given in the lectures, there are not many specially prepared case studies on important policy issues, which can be used to provide experiential learning. Some of the long-term educational programs in the USA, such as at Pittsburgh University, have been asking groups of students to work on live policy issues coming before the legislature and to present their analysis to real-life decision makers in the absence of local case studies. Case studies from countries similarly placed could be used, but experience shows that, with groups of very senior officials, such case studies from other environments are not effective.

Another method of bringing realism into the classroom is through inviting experienced policy makers, policy analysts and critics of certain policies as guest lecturers. At the Indian Institute of Public Administration, New Delhi these also included journalists and politicians from different political parties. Such a training program provides a good opportunity for national leaders to sensitize senior administrators to some of the important policy issues of national significance. Work visits not only break the monotony of the classroom environment but also add realism to the learning process. However, in the context of a training program for senior administrators, these visits need to be specially selected and prepared. Visits to institutions and places which are relevant for policy making but with which normally the civic servants are not confronted in their day-to-day work, are important in this connection. Visits to important private sector organizations, policy research institutions, interest group organizations and offices of opposition parties may sensitize administrators to a different kind of policy reaction than they are used to in their official interactions.

An interesting method of self-study tried in the Hyderabad programme is to ask each participant to write a review of a book from the library, approved by the course coordinator. This compels the busy administrator to look at the world of research and academia seriously and then give his 'hard-boiled' reaction based on his robust practical experience. Another method which may prove useful in the case of a country where, as yet, very little local capacity in training and research in this area exists is to take the group on a study visit to another country where advanced training in policy analysis exists and where practice of policy analysis may have been reorganized as a result of certain administrative reforms. This is expensive, but the motivational importance of such a method is tremendous, as is the willingness to look at policy problems of others critically. This is very much recommended for the very top levels of the civil service.

Staffing Short-term Courses

In general, the running of short-term courses does not require a large resident faculty, but because of the complex nature of the courses in public policy requiring expert advice in a variety of fields and in order to provide inputs from different disciplines, a number of senior, experienced teachers/researchers need to be available during such a course. This is very important for maintaining the motivation of the participants. This does not pose a problem in a university, where such staff may be readily available. If the course is organized by specialized training institution, it has to ensure that during the period of the program a core of regular and guest faculty members is available, not only for specific lectures and guidance on syndicate and project work, but also to provide a sounding board for the exploratory policy analysis of participants.

Both in Manila and Hyderabad there was a core faculty of staff from different disciplines, supplemented by a large number of guest lecturers. In the intensive one-week policy analysis workshop run by Dror, all teaching was done by one person, which could be strenuous both for the course leader and for the participants.

Literature Used

Teaching of public policy in developing countries, both in the long-term educational programs and in short-term courses, is handicapped by lack of sufficient literature on different aspects of policy making, especially of an empirical nature. Often teachers are forced to use standard references from the USA and Europe and adjust them for use in their own countries. This is not satisfactory. The reality of policy making in developing countries is often so different from the picture of the institutionalized, pluralistic policy-making scene of many western countries (Richard Hofferbert, 'What Social

Scientists Do Not Know About Public Policies in Poor Countries', paper presented to the XIIIth World Congress of International Political Science Association, Paris, 15–20 July 1985) that, after making adjustments, very little of the original framework may remain. The *Bibliography of References on Policymaking in Developing Countries* which has been compiled by the project director can be used to select particular references, to be supplemented by readings on the local situation.

In view of the newness of training in this area and the high profile of the expected clientele, prior research by a team of staff members who would be responsible for organizing such a course is highly recommended. Such research should not only establish the contents of such a training program, but should also aim at preparing specific teaching materials, including case studies, based on the local situation. Using consultants with the proper background and experience may be desirable in the beginning.

Member institutions desirous of having more information can contact the institutions whose experiences have been reported in this chapter of the project director himself.

Contents of Some Short-term Training Courses in Public Policy for Senior Administrators

Yehezkel Dror (Organized in different places)

Module I	Introduction to policy analysis and planning
Module II	Predictions, forecasting and handling of uncertainty and complexity
Module III	Simulation and gaming
Module IV	Cost–benefit analysis, micro-economics, alternative evaluation, social experimentation and value analysis
Module V	Applied history and multiple perspective
Module VI	Decision psychology, organizational behavior, bureaucratic politics
Module VII	Advanced policy analysis of complex issues
Model VIII	Upgrading of decision-making systems

Philippines (College of Public Administration, Manila)

Module 1: role of analysis in policy formulation
A   General field of public policy
B   Policy research for formulation and implementation
C   Models for policy analysis

D   Programme management, evaluation and policy evaluation
E   Model of choice, ends of policy, public goods concept

Module 2: methods and tools of policy analysis
A   Systems analysis
B   Overview methods of policy analysis
C   Quantitative tools
       regression modeling
       differential equations
       linear programing
       exploratory data analysis
       cost–benefit modeling
       forecasting projections
       decision analysis
       computer applications, simulations
D   Qualitative tools
       Delphi
       scenario writing
       syndicate work
       implementation analysis

Hyderabad (Administrative Staff College)

Topics in order of participants' preference:
1   Leadership
2   Executive stress
3   Project management techniques
4   Role analysis
5   Social audit
6   Management by objective
7   Investment planning
8   Public policy process
9   Global economy
10 Decision-making styles
11 Product market strategies
12 Group dynamics
13 India and World Bank
14 Quality circles
15 Determinates of development
16 Indices of development
17 Work culture
18 Industry and environment

19 Privatization: industry, trade, finance
20 Industrialization development
21 Group decisions
22 Social responsibility of industry
23 Management science
24 Probability theory
25 Ethics in public administration
26 Export promotion policy
27 Energy management for industry
28 Sources of finance
29 Japanese–Indian management
30 Corporate turnaround
31 Time management
32 Industrial relations
33 Indian economy
34 Social cost–benefit modeling
35 Industry transport bottlenecks
36 Cybernetics
37 Zerobase budgeting
38 Strategic planning
39 Image analysis
40 Data base for policy process
41 Yoga
42 Policy planning process
43 Use of pcs

11 USIA Win–Win Traveling Seminars

Regarding the USIA traveling seminars dealing with conflict resolution in South Asia and elsewhere, the key *general ideas* are as follows.

1 The world can be divided into the five continents of Africa, Asia, Europe, Latin America and North America. Each continent can then be divided into approximately six regions sharing a common geography and possibly a common language or culture. Appendix 1 roughly divides the developing world into 24 regions for the purpose of conducting workshops or traveling seminars.
2 Each traveling seminar can include a leading authority from each country within the region. Those authorities will generally be professors teaching political or social science, since those are the issues to be emphasized. The authorities can be referred to as the presenters, since each seminar will begin with their brief presentations.
3 The traveling seminar can spend at least one day in each country within each region. The roundtable participants or discussants may consist of leading academics, journalists and government people from the country or countries where the traveling seminars occur.
4 The topic of each traveling seminar will be something like 'US Policy with _____ in the 90s and Beyond', with the name of the region inserted.
5 A key purpose of the seminar will be to clarify how policies can be developed that are mutually beneficial for the United States and the countries of the region. Such policies can also be developed between countries and groups within the region, and also with international organizations that involve the region.
6 This mutuality purpose will draw upon ideas from win–win dispute resolution, super-optimizing policy analysis and related conflict resolution ideas. The moderator for the traveling seminars should be someone

well versed and experienced in such methods, but not one who is considered an authority on the region.

Format, Implementation and Feedback

The *general format* involves the following steps:

1 opening remarks from the USIA and the moderator;
2 brief presentations from the authorities addressed to the topic of the seminar (allow for a total of about 120 minutes: each speaker gets 120/N minutes where N is the number of speakers);
3 the moderator summarizes the points of agreement and disagreement among the presenters;
4 the participants raise questions and make comments for at least 60 minutes before breaking for lunch;
5 the presenters then offer a reappraisal of their original presentations in light of the questions and comments that have been raised (allow for a total of about 60 minutes: each speaker gets 60/N minutes);
6 allow at least 60 minutes of further questions and comments in light of the reappraisals;
7 the moderator summarizes new points of agreement and disagreement; the moderator also provides integration and comments concerning procedures for possible resolution of the points of disagreement;
8 the presenters and discussants react to the moderator's summary with further questions, comments, suggestions and rebuttals;
9 the USIA host says a few parting words, followed by a cocktail reception.

As for the implementation of the *substantive ideas* in South Asia, the following items were distributed and discussed:

1 a copy of the agenda for the traveling seminar that was held in Bombay, see the 9–point format discussed above;
2 a causal arrow diagram, entitled 'US Policy and Economic, Political and Military Matters in Developing and Industrialized Nations', which was used to summarize the morning presentations and discussion, see Figure 11.1;
3 an international flow chart, entitled 'US Policy Over Time Toward Developing and Industrialized Nations', which was used to summarize the afternoon reappraisals and discussion, see Figure 11.2.

As regards the implementation of the *procedural ideas* in South Asia, the following items were distributed and discussed:

1 the chapter on 'Super-Optimizing Analysis and Policy Studies' from S. Nagel and Miriam Mills, *Professional Development in Policy Studies* (Greenwood, 1993);
2 an application of the ideas presented in the article to the economic problem of 'Trade Versus Aid in South Asia and Elsewhere', see Table 11.3, Row 1;
3 an application to the political problem of 'Secession in South Asia and Elsewhere', see Table 11.3, Row 2;
4 an application to the military problem of 'Having Nuclear Weapons in South Asia and Elsewhere', see Table 11.3, Row 3.

The *feedback* for the three traveling seminars conducted in New Delhi, Sri Lanka and Bombay has been quite favorable:

1 The USIA members who participated most actively in the three seminars all praised them. They included Richard Scorza of New Delhi, William Maurer of Sri Lanka and Roger Rosco of Bombay.
2 The presenters also indicated that they were quite pleased at the farewell dinner, which was held in Bombay. The presenters included Professor Pervais Cheema of Pakistan, Shelton Kodikara of Sri Lanka and S.D. Muni of India.
3 The seminar also received favorable comments from the participants in all three places. These comments referred to the conflict resolution purposes of the seminar, as well as the South Asia substance.

Win–Win US Foreign Policy

The leading controversial issues in developing nations like those of South Asia tend to be economic, political and military issues: the economic issues relate to ways to make domestic economies more prosperous and how to facilitate investments, exports and imports; the political issues relate to promoting democratic institutions, human rights and self-determination; the military issues relate to non-proliferation of arms and reduction of regional conflicts.

The first six causal relations in Figure 11.1 can be interpreted as follows: (1) reduction of military conflicts is conducive to prosperity and investment; (2) prosperity is conducive to reduction of military conflicts, especially prosperity based on buying and selling across countries that might otherwise be in

136 *Policy Within and Across Developing Nations*

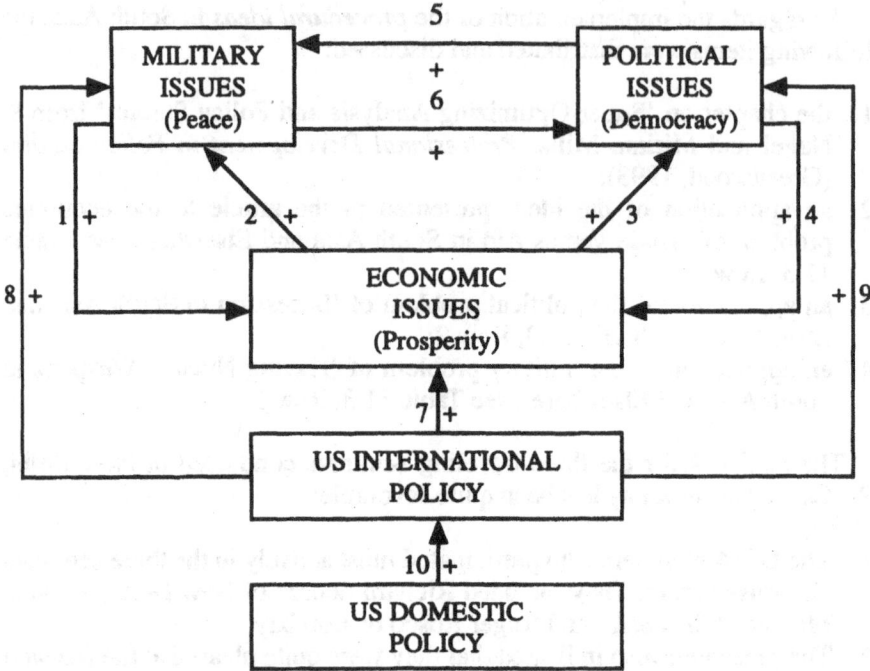

Figure 11.1 Win–win US foreign policy

conflict; (3) prosperity is conducive to democratic institutions, human rights and tolerance of minority ethnic groups; (4) democracy, human rights and ethnic peace are conducive to prosperity; (5) democratic political institutions are also conducive to a reduction of military conflicts; and (6) reducing military conflicts is also conducive to democratic political institutions.

The last four causal relations can be interpreted as follows: (7) US policy is concerned with encouraging prosperity, investment, exporting and importing because doing so is mutually beneficial; (8) US policy is concerned with reducing military conflicts partly because of the favorable effect on prosperity and the economic issues; (9) US policy is concerned with promoting a democratic political environment partly because of the favorable effect on prosperity and the economic issues; and (10) US domestic economic policy emphasizes US prosperity and GNP growth which partly explains why US international policy emphasizes mutually beneficial trade and investment opportunities.

A number of miscellaneous points should be made. First, in the context of South Asia, Pakistan is especially concerned with military security, India is especially concerned with political issues and Sri Lanka is especially concerned with international economics, but all three countries are concerned with all three sets of issues. Second, the concept of mutual benefit is promoted through regional organizations, such as the South Asia Association for Regional Cooperation, as well as through interregional interaction between South Asia and the USA. Third, social issues such as poverty and ethnic groups are also important, although they were considered under economic and political issues, respectively. Technology issues are also quite important, but they were discussed in the context of military, economic and political issues. Finally, there are positive relations among all five variables shown in Figure 11.1 as shown by the plus sign. These relations are positive in the sense of upward causation and being desirable relations, especially regarding promotion of peace, prosperity and democracy. Upward causation means the variables lower in the figure cause, determine or influence the variables higher in the figure although there is also reciprocal feedback causation.

Past US Foreign Policy

The past was characterized by colonialism and the cold war. The present is being characterized by investment, importing and exporting of funds and food. The future may be characterized by transfer of technologies and skills from the USA which results in mutually beneficial investment returns, buying and selling. See Figure 11.2. The arrows from the *past* indicate: (1 & 2) colonialism involved low wages going to the developing nations and valuable resources going to the United States or other industrialized nations; (3 & 4) the cold war involved arms and aid going to developing nations and allegiance going to the USA or the Soviet Union.

The arrows from the *present* indicate: (5 & 6) capital investment going to the developing nations with a reasonable return going back to the United States; (7 & 8) cash or credits going to developing nations in return for their products; (9 & 10) products going to developing nations in return for their cash or credits.

The arrows from the *future* indicate: (11 & 12) technologies and skill going to developing nations, thereby improving their ability to be good places for investment, buying and selling.

In the past, there was often an imbalance, with disproportionate benefits to the industrial nations and disproportionate detriments to the developing nations. In the present, there are generally mutual benefits from investment, exporting and importing. In the future, the transfer of technologies and skills may enable all participating countries to exceed their best initial expectations simultaneously.

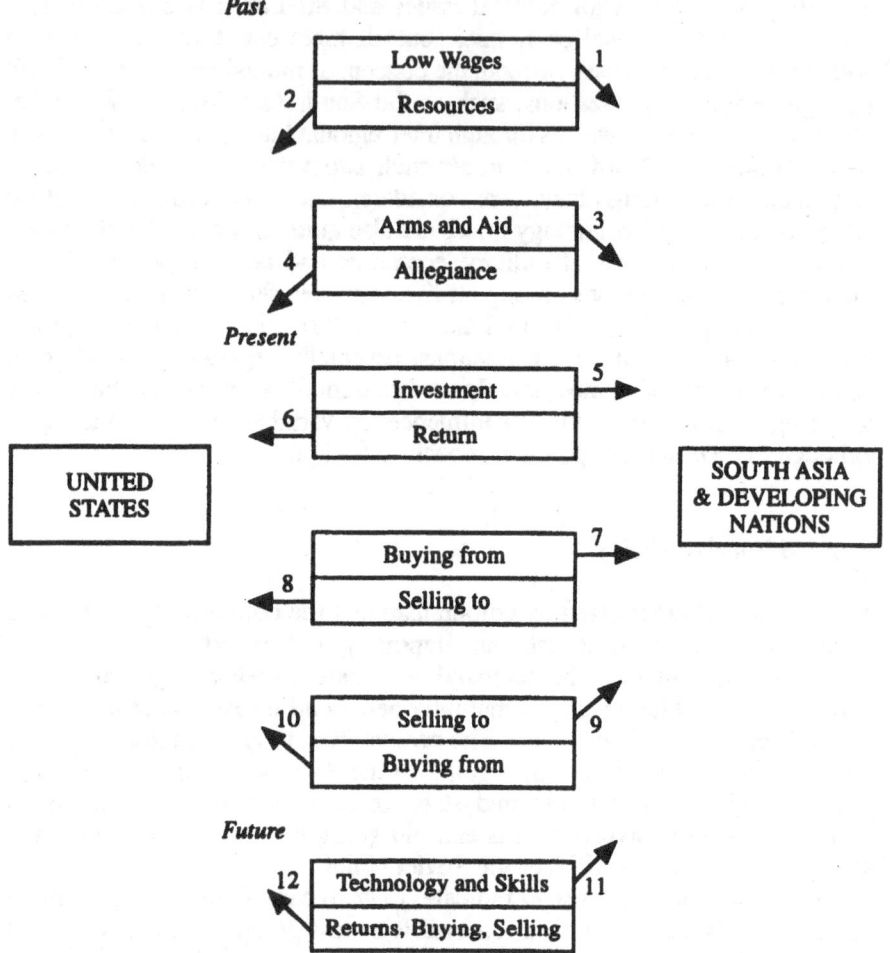

Figure 11.2 US foreign policy for 200 years

Win–Win Issues in South Asia

Trade versus Aid (Table 11.1, Row 1)

The United States currently tends to favor trade over aid, since trade is more mutually beneficial than aid which tends mainly to benefit the recipient nation unless there is a cold war return. Developing nations have tended to favor aid with no strings attached in the past, since they are fearful that

Table 11.1 Win–win issues in South Asia

Issues	Pro-US position	Pro-South Asia position	Neutral or compromise	Win–win or SOS
1 Trade versus aid in South Asia	1 Mainly trade	1 Mainly aid	1 Some trade 2 Some aid	1 Skills transfer 2 Technology transfer
2 Secession in South Asia (Kashmir)	1 Self-determination	1 Retain rebellious provinces (pro-India) 2 Release rebellious provinces (pro-Pakistan)	1 Partition	1 Autonomy like that of a US state
3 Nuclear arms in South Asia	1 No nuclear arms	1 Retain the capability that exists	1 Reduce 2 Inspect	1 Peaceful conversion

buying from the United States will disrupt local industries, and that they have little to sell the United States.

Skills and technology transfer greatly benefits the United States by virtue of improving places for US investment, the buying of American products, and the selling to the United States of products needed by the American people. Skills and technology transfer benefits developing nations, even more than offering them either trade or aid, by enabling them to upgrade their international competitiveness.

Seceding (Table 11.1, Row 2)

The United States tends to favor self-determination out of a regard for democratic decision making and emphasizing the majority will within the rebellious provinces. Developing nations tend to favor retaining their own rebellious provinces, emphasizing the majority will within the larger political entity. Autonomy like that of a US state refers to states having their own constitutions and governors that cannot be removed by Washington: states in India do not have their own constitutions and their governors can be removed by New Delhi.

Nuclear Arms (Table 11.1, Row 3)

The United States tends to favor removal of nuclear arms from South Asia for fear that their presence may lead to nuclear warfare which might involve the United States directly or indirectly by way of the international disruption. Countries like India and Pakistan which have nuclear capability are reluctant to weaken their deterrent power against each other.

Peaceful conversion in this context means providing India and Pakistan with the skills and technologies for converting their nuclear capability into peaceful and safe nuclear energy, along with American investment funding.

Appendix 1
PSO World Regions

I. **Africa Workshops**
   Arabic–speaking North Africa
   French–speaking West Africa
   English–speaking West Africa
   English–speaking East Africa
   English–speaking Southern Africa
   French– and Portuguese–speaking Southern Africa

II. **Asia Workshops**
   China and neighboring Mongolia and North Korea
   South Asia, including India and Pakistan
   Southeast Asia, including Malaysia, Indochina, Thailand, Indonesia, and the Philippines
   West Asia, including the Asian countries west of Pakistan
   The relatively industrialized countries of East Asia from Japan to New Zealand
   The Asian part of the former Soviet Union

III. **Latin America Workshops**
   The Southern Cone, including Argentina and Chile
   Brazil, as a region in itself
   Central South America, from Paraguay through Peru
   Northern South America, including Colombia and Venezuela
   The Caribbean, including Cuba, Haiti, and the other islands
   Central America, from Panama through Mexico

IV. **Europe Workshops**
   The European part of the former Soviet Union
   The southern part of East Europe, from former Yugoslavia through Greece
   The central part of East Europe, from Austria through Rumania

142 *Policy Within and Across Developing Nations*

       The northern part of East Europe, from Poland through Scandinavia
       The northern half of West Europe, but emphasizing OECD and EU activities toward developing nations, with the Institute of Social Studies at The Hague as a meeting site
       The southern half of West Europe, with the Developmental Studies Program at the University of Bologna as a meeting site

V. **Topical Workshops**
       Economic policy, for promoting prosperity
       Social policy, for promoting equal opportunity
       Science policy, for promoting technology improvement
       Political policy, for promoting democracy
       International policy, for promoting peace
       Legal policy, for promoting law compliance

12   Proposed Policy Analysis Training Program

The venue for a proposed policy analysis training program will be the National School of Administration at the People's University in Beijing under the direction of the successor to Professor Huang Da-qiang. The National School should have its own facilities built near the People's University in time to host the training program. An alternative venue might be the Department of International Politics at Beijing University. The National School, however, has the advantage of better bridging academics and practitioners. The best time for the program would be about June 1998. June is a desirable month because instructors from various universities can more easily attend since their classes are not likely to be in session. June is also less hot than the later summer months. Those invited should consist of instructors of public administration, political science and related subjects who have an interest in systematic public policy evaluation. They should include those who offer courses within government agencies, as well as within universities.

The presentations will be in either English or Chinese. Simultaneous translation with earphones will be provided. This will enable Chinese-speaking participants to hear the English presentations in Chinese. There will also be knowledgeable interpreters available to supplement the simultaneous translation. Knowledgeable in this context refers to a knowledge of public policy analysis as well as an ability to translate English into Chinese, and vice versa.

Books, articles and other assigned readings will be translated before the sessions begin. The printed or duplicated translations will be made available to the participants so that they can be read prior to and during the sessions. Relevant books, which will emphasize systematic public policy evaluation, may include S. Nagel, *Public Policy: Goals, Means and Methods* (St Martin's, 1984) and Edward Quade, *Analysis for Public Decisions* (North-Holland, 1989). Video tapes will be made of the sessions so that people who cannot attend them can use the tapes as a partial substitute.

The training program will include teaching the participants how to use decision-aiding software in public policy evaluation. Decision-aiding software is software or methods for processing a set of goals to be achieved, alternatives available for achieving them and relations between goals and alternatives in order to choose or explain the best alternative, combination, allocation or predictive decision rule. The program is expected to last about three weeks and it will involve meeting all morning to participate in lectures and discussions. The afternoons will make use of individual tutorial study to apply the software to specific policy problems in which each participant is interested.

The availability of the training program will be publicized in advance by relevant associations such as the Chinese Administration Society under the direction of Secretary-General Liu Yichang. The program will be jointly sponsored by the public administration and political science departments of Beijing University, Zhongshan University and other major universities. An advisory board should be established consisting of relevant people from the universities, such as Professor Bao-Xu Zhao of Beijing University and Professor Shuzhang Xia of Zhongshan University. The sponsorship should also include training institutes within the government, such as the Institute of Management of the Ministry of Machinery and Electronics under Dean Shi Lichuan and the Institute of Administration for Guangdong Province under the direction of Professor Li Huajie.

One major activity of the participants should be to plan the development of a Chinese Policy Studies Organization analogous to the PSO in the United States. The participants should be grouped for group work according to the public policy problems in which they are most interested, such as public policy toward defense, crime, economic development, education, labor–management relations, health care, environmental protection, energy or international diplomacy. The work with decision-aiding software will involve 'hands-on' experience. There should be about one computer for every five participants in the training program. The participants will be provided with software. The participants will work on projects relevant to their interests. The instructor will arrange for the publication of a set of the applications in the Policy Studies Organization Series of Macmillan Press.

In circulating publicity concerning the training course, suggestions will be sought from potential participants as to how the course might be made even more useful to their interests. Participants in the program can form an alumni group and issue a periodic newsletter informing members of the group of new developments in the literature, the software and the applications.

If the initial course in 1998 is successful, an updated version can be offered every few years thereafter. It should not be necessary for Americans to offer this same course again because the original participants can spread the word regarding the methods taught in their capacities as public administration instructors at universities or government agencies. In other words, this 1998 course is designed to train the trainers, who can then offer courses workshops, seminars and other teaching programs for training other trainers without needing as much outside input as in the beginning.

It is anticipated that the Asia Foundation will be a chief source of funding for this training program. Other partial sources of funding might include universities, government agencies and other foundations in the United States, and universities and government agencies in China.

As a prerequisite to conducting this policy analysis program in China, it is anticipated that conditions will become more conducive to freedom of speech, the free exchange of ideas and constructive criticism of governmental policy. Effective, efficient and equitable public policy evaluation cannot exist unless these conditions are present. An atmosphere hospitable to innovative ideas may exist in Chinese universities and in most government agencies. If, however, the government at the top is perceived to be openly hostile to constructive criticism, the program should be indefinitely postponed. The trends in China since at least 1980 have been in the direction of encouraging higher education, more professionalism and innovative ideas. It is sincerely hoped that the events of June 1989 represent a temporary setback which will be overcome by those longer trends by 1998.

As of 1997 China seems poised for big changes. It has recently undergone very big changes regarding the establishment of competition among business firms in the economy. That is like the perestroika capitalism which Gorbachev instituted in the Soviet Union, although it was instituted in the PRC by Deng Xioping. China may be about to adopt some new forms of competition in the political realm, comparable to the glasnost free speech which Gorbachev instituted, although it may be instituted under the new PRC leader Jiang Zemin.

China has been able to justify a series of dictators or autocrats ever since prehistoric times for roughly the following reasons:

1. The emperors justified their autocracy on the need to unite the feudal nation or empire against invaders from the north, which is why there is a Great Wall in China.
2. After 1911, Sun Yat-Sen justified his supposedly temporary autocracy as needed to consolidate the revolution against the remnants of the Manchu feudalism.
3. After the passing of Sun Yat-Sen, Chiang Kai-shek justified his autocracy on the need to suppress the provincial warlords and then the invasion from Japan.

4 After Chiang Kai-shek was expelled, Mao Zedong justified his autocracy on the need to deal with the cold war, especially the perceived threat from the United States and also the need to build a collectivist economy and culture.
5 After Mao died, Deng Xioping could justify his autocracy in light of the continuing cold war, friction with Russia, the shift to capitalism and exaggerated fears of student rebellion.

As of 1997, the cold war is over. Neither the US nor Russia is threatening. Capitalism has been successfully established under the ironic direction of the Communist Party. The students are not so rebellious, partly because they are anticipating peaceful change. The country is in the hands of an engineer, rather than a veteran of the Long March which is the Chinese equivalent of being a Bolshevik veteran of the 1917 revolution. That makes Jiang Zemin like Gorbachev. Jiang is also an engineer and the first prime minister who is not an old Bolshevik. Jiang Zemin is the former mayor of cosmopolitan Shanghai with strong labor union support. He thus has a personal background and an historical environment that is conducive toward announcing the kinds of changes which Gorbachev instituted in the political realm.

What might those changes be? For one thing, China has a system of provincial governors and city mayors who are appointed by Beijing. That could easily be changed to allow the people in the provinces and the cities to elect their own chief executives, as is done in virtually all major countries of the world. Electing those chief executives would mean that people would be nominated by groups and that would-be candidates would seek group support. That would especially mean the possibility of some candidates running who are not official Communist Party candidates. Most of the candidates would at first be from the Communist Party since it is the strongest and best organized group. Giving the voters some choice in the elections would be a foot in the door that would probably soon open to a competitive political system like the competitive economy.

Such competition can lead to candidates competing to see who can offer the best ideas and do the best job of implementing ideas. That kind of competition can be even more important to a successful society than competition among business firms, although both forms of competition are important. Political and economic competition together lead to long-term high prosperity. China is presently doing well without formal political competition, but could probably be doing even better with it. Possibly more important, political competition may be inevitable in all modern industrial countries. This is so because industrial countries require an educated population. Such people eventually rebel against being dictated to in the political realm, as has happened in West Europe starting with the French Revolution, and more recently East Europe.

We could end this book (with the exception of the bibliographic chapters) on that high optimistic note. Realistic optimism, however, should emphasize that so-called inevitable occurrences may not occur unless concerned people vigorously pursue them. This may include the American president and the European Community who need to put more economic pressure on China to accelerate its evolution toward competitive democratic politics. The Chinese students may also need to exert new pressure, including the sons and daughters of Community Party leaders. The children of both Deng Xioping and Jiang Zemin have gone to American universities. The Communist Party leadership has sons and daughters at People's University in Beijing and other universities, where they were among the most active leaders in the pro-democracy movement of 1989. They are now moving up in government positions. China is also opening up to world literature, television and movies which have a pro-democratic influence. Some day soon, China will probably follow Russia into joining the Big Eight as a reasonably democratic economic power.

PART IV
RELEVANT BIBLIOGRAPHIES

13 Developmental Policy Studies: The Relevant Literature

Robert W. Hunt

Over the past two decades, third world countries have attempted increasingly to deal with staggering economic problems through policy changes. In this they have been strongly encouraged by the international aid and lending community. The major purposes of the policy changes have been economic stabilization and the promotion of growth through structural adjustments. These changes have been controversial and their impacts widely debated. However, major donors continued, for a long time, to perceive structural adjustment and the policies that support it as the most appropriate mechanisms for promoting development.

Criticisms of this approach to development have stressed the difficulties with the 'received wisdom' of major bilateral and multi-lateral development programs. Many critics have focused on the need to find ways to promote and sustain policy dialogues among the major participants in development programs, including the poor. Central to these arguments are concerns for institutional capacity, particularly for those institutions responsible for designing, managing and sustaining developmental changes. Developmental agencies, including the US Agency for International Development and the World Bank, have begun to accept this critique, which has its intellectual base in institutional economics and public choice theory.

Alternative critiques of development theory and development policy have come, over the past two decades, from students and advocates of voluntary organizations for, and of, the poorest members of societies. They have expressed doubts about policies for national economic planning and modernization, and about the increased attention to governance and institutions. They focus on empowerment, popular participation and 'micro-policy' networks as development mechanisms. Their policies of 'bubble up' (as opposed to 'trickle down') have served to define a strongly populist alternative for development programing and transformation. A more dramatic version of this alternative is represented in the heritage of Gandhian visions of society, which has promoted strong doubts about the very values of development, even among those seeking to serve the poorest and promote their participation. Many scholars and practitioners with these perspectives choose to emphasize the historical context, languages and myths of societies, while asking more open-ended questions about their future. By expressing less certainty about political institutions and public development policies, they leave open the possibility that small, alternative communities, more autonomous and authentic, may become alternative foci for societies in transition. A synthesis of these views may be emerging through the implicit recognition of two related paradoxes. First is the 'orthodox paradox', suggesting that with efforts to privatize the economy comes a companion need for more effective, rather than diminished, government capacity. Such an increased capacity would mean not only more effective policy making and implementation by public agencies, but an enhanced capability for integrating the public at large in the policy process.

A second 'populist paradox' offers a parallel logic: that free and autonomous citizenship commonly requires enhanced governmental authority. A meeting point for these two arguments is the 'civil society', that set of mediating institutions which reflect public goals and needs and are engaged in the political process, but autonomous from it. A well institutionalized civil society would encompass these polarities and could serve as an autonomous bridge linking public and government for dialogues on political and economic development. Proponents argue that such mediating institutions could promote fundamental critiques of development assumptions and values, and the consideration of alternative development policies and programs rooted in indigenous traditions and meanings.

This bibliography is part of the preparation work for editing a volume on economic development in the multi-volume treatise on *Policy Studies and Developing Nations* (JAI Press, 1998). This volume will touch on these competing approaches to development policy making and implementation, offering case studies and comparative research on the strengths, weaknesses and potential of each. Analyses of broadly based macrostructural changes would be followed by those looking at participatory institutions, and the role of popular participation in the promotion of policy alternatives. The concluding section would focus on the polarities reflected in the discussions in the first sections, and provide analyses of the implications of an emergent civil order for broadly based economic policy formulation and implementation.

Restructuring Distressed Economies: Policy Reform and its Impacts

Since the late 1970s, the stress in international development assistance programs has been on macroeconomic policy reform within developing nations. These reforms were to be directed at establishing the importance of market forces in setting prices and production goals, expanding trade and improving the climate for entrepreneurial activity. In the wake of experiences and criticisms, these stabilization and structural adjustment programs have evolved, with more attention now being given to issues of environmental balance and sustainability, and to the emergence of better managed, adaptable institution in the public and private sectors. Still the 'received wisdom' of the World Bank and other influential assistance agencies continues to stress the need to establish market mechanisms as the centerpiece of decision making on development issues. Critics, some within the World Bank and other major assistance agencies, have argued for greater attention to the institutional context for development, most recently including the political system and policy-making process in that recommendation. The basically technocratic perspective on development policy making remains.

Bibliography

Bhatnagar, Bhuvan and Aubrey C. Williams (eds), 'Part Development and the World Bank: Potential Directions for Change' (draft manuscript) (World Bank, n.d.).

Cornia, Giovanni, Richard Jolly and Francis Stewart (eds), *Adjustment with a Human Face: Protecting the Vulnerable and Promoting Growth*, Vol. 1 (Clarendon Press, 1987).

Cowan, L.G., 'A Global Overview of Privatization', in S.H. Hanke (ed.), *Privatization and Development* (Institute for Contemporary Studies, 1987).

Gereffi, Gary and Donald L. Wyman (eds), *Manufacturing Miracles: Paths of Industrialization in Latin America and East Asia* (Princeton University Press, 1990).

Graham, Lawrence and Robert H. Wilson (eds), *The Political Economy of Brazil: Public Policies in an Era of Transition* (University of Texas Press, 1990).

Havnevik, Kjell (ed.), *The IMF and the World Bank in Africa: Conditionally, Impact and Alternatives* (Scandinavian Institute of African Studies, 1987).

Israel, Arturo, *Institutional Development: Incentives to Performance* (Johns Hopkins University Press, 1987).

Mosely, Paul, Jane Harrigan and John Toye, *AID and Power: The World Bank and Policy Based Lending*, Vol. 1, (Routledge, 1991).

Nelson, Joan, *Economic Crisis and Policy Choice: The Politics of Adjustment in the Third World* (Princeton University Press, 1990).
Stewart, Frances, 'The Many Faces of Adjustment', **19**, *World Development*, 12, 1847–64 (December 1991).
Thomas, Vinod, Ajay Chhibber, Mansoor Dailami and Jaime de Melo (eds), *Restructuring Economies in Distress: Policy Reform and the World Bank* (Oxford University Press, 1991).
United Nations Economic Commission for Africa, *African Alternative Framework to Structural Adjustment Programmes for Socio-Economic Recovery and Transformation* (United Nations, 1985).
World Bank, *World Development Report, 1991* (Oxford University Press, 1991).

Political Institutions as the Missing Component in Adjustment Programs: Perspectives on their Source and Impact

Critics of stabilization and structural adjustment programs have concluded that the institutional base of development has been undervalued in these programs. They differ, however, in the choice of institutions most needing improvement. The top economists and development professionals of the World Bank might well focus on the need to improve management skills in the public and private sectors, but certainly in the planning and implementing agencies of government. They seek to improve public capacity for setting a framework for competition and expansion, and improving efficiency – in part by limiting corruption. Other critics, some from the 'voluntary sector', and from among those with backgrounds in political science and anthropology, have tended to argue for more attention to citizen groups and to the expansion of planning and management capabilities from the bottom of society. For some, a kind of democratic response to central economic and political authority and macroeconomic planning has dominated. They bring arguments from Gandhi and other populist, even anarchistic, thinking to bear in assessing the institutional response to 'modernization'. Most of these critics, however, focus on the need to mobilize the poorest for participation in the wider community – as empowered, active citizens.

Bibliography

Chazan, Naomi, 'Africa's Democratic Challenge', **9**, *World Policy Journal*, 2, 279–307 (Spring, 1992).
Clark, John, *Democratizing Development: The Role of Voluntary Organizations* (Kumarian Press, 1991).

Durning, Alan, *Action at the Grassroots: Fighting Poverty and Environmental Decline*, Worldwatch Paper no. 88 (Worldwatch Institute, 1989).

Edgcomb, Elaine and James Cawley, 'The Process of Institutional Development: Assisting Small Enterprise Institutions to Become More Effective', GEMINI Working Paper No. 15 (US Agency for International Development, February 1991).

Heilman, Lawrence C. and Robert J. Kurz, 'Democratic Initiatives Performance Monitoring Study for the Latin America and Caribbean Bureau', prepared for US Agency for International Development, Latin America Bureau (Management Systems International, January, 1991).

Hellinger, Stephen, Douglas Hellinger and Fred O'Regan, *AID for Just Development: Report on the Future of Foreign Assistance* (Lynne Rienner, 1988). (A study which focuses on the means for institutionalizing relations among non-governmental organizations and the political system in developing nations.)

Kaviraj, Sudipta, 'On the State, Society and Discourse in India', in J. Manor (ed.), *Rethinking Third World Politics* (Longmans, 1991, pp. 72–99).

Korten, David, 'Micro-Policy Reform – The Role of Private Voluntary Agencies', in David Korten (ed.), *Community Management: Asian Experiences and Perspectives* (Kumarian Press, 1986).

Lewis, John et al., *Strengthening the Poor: What Have We Learned?* (Transaction Books, 1988).

Mann, Charles, Merilee Grindle and Parker Shipton, *Seeking Solutions: Framework and Cases for Small Enterprise Development Programs* (Kumarian Press, 1989). (A summary of lessons learned from a five-year US government program to analyze the institutional bases for successful business enterprise and community development programs.)

Migdal, Joel, *Strong Societies and Weak States* (Princeton University Press, 1988).

Nandy, Ashis, 'From Outside the Imperium: Gandhi's Cultural Critique of the West', in A. Nandy (ed.), *Traditions, Tyranny and Utopias: Essays in the Politics of Awareness* (Oxford University Press, 1987).

Picciotto, Robert, 'Participatory Development: Myths and Dilemmas', World Bank Policy Research Working Papers (World Bank, July 1992).

Schimpp, Michele Wozniak, 'A.I.D. and Democratic Development: A Synthesis of Literature and Experience' (Agency for International Development, Center for Development Information and Evaluation, May 1992).

Schneider, Bertrand, *The Barefoot Revolution: A Report to the Club of Rome* (Intermediate Technology Publications, 1988).

Uphoff, Norman, *Local Institutional Development: An Analytic Sourcebook with Cases* (Kumarian Press, 1986).

Uphoff, Norman, 'Assisted Self-Reliance: Working With, Rather than For,

the Poor', in John Lewis *et al.*, *Strengthening the Poor: What Have We Learned?* (Transaction Books, 1988, pp. 47–59).
White, Louise, *Implementing Policy Change in LDCs: A Strategy for Designing and Effecting Change* (Lynne Rienner, 1990).
World Bank, *Managing Development: The Governance Dimension* (World Bank, 1991).

Dialogues and Dialectics: New Synthesis in a Civil Society

While critiques of macroeconomic policy making have had an impact, they have not resolved the dimensions on how to proceed. Macroeconomic planners continue to believe that 'add-ons' which deal with excesses of privatization and structural change will provide sufficient amelioration for those who are most harmed by these changes. Planners who seek to promote more effective governance are challenged by the size of their task and the uncertain impacts of reforms which may or may not articulate with the wider social setting. Populists, with their focus on small groups and community activism, are challenged to show how small changes can be promoted and sustained in a cost-effective way and replicated throughout the society so that benefits and changes do not promote regional tensions.

One tentative answer comes from theory and research on democratic development, and from investigations of the 'civil order' within societies in change. Can a dialectical process be promoted and supported so as to allow for the emergence of larger and larger policy networks? Can these 'bridge' networks provide, with different responses in different settings, the appropriate balance between local initiative and responsibility, on the one hand, and national, even international, policy processes, on the other? What does the evidence show?

Bibliography

Annis, Sheldon, 'Can Small Scale Development be Large State Policy?', in S. Annis and P. Hamim (eds), *Direct to the Poor. Grassroots Development in Latin America* (Lynne Rienner, 1988, pp. 209–18).
Bratton, Michael, 'Beyond the State: Civil Society and Associational Life in Africa', **41**, *World Politics*, 3 (407–30, 1989).
Carroll, Thomas, *Intermediary NGOS: the Supporting Link in Grassroots Development* (Kumarian Press, 1992).
Gohlert, Ernst, *Power and Culture: The Struggle Against Poverty in Thailand* (White Lotus, 1991).
Holt, Sharon L., 'Village Banking: A Cross-Country Study of a Community

Based Lending Methodology', (US Agency for International Development, Bureau for Asia and Private Enterprise, December 1991). (Holt's work is an evaluation of several varieties of village banks in developing countries. She reports on efforts to 'scale up' these projects and to promote a wider range of political activity by the poor, and a policy dialogue between the political leaders and the public.)

Kaviraj, Sudipta, 'On the State, Society and Discourse in India', in J. Manor (ed.), *Rethinking Third World Politics* (Longmans, 1991, pp. 72–99).

Korten, David, *Getting to the Twenty-first Century: Voluntary Action and the Global Agenda* (Kumarian Press, 1990).

Lovell, Catherine, *Breaking the Cycle of Poverty: The Bangladesh Rural Advancement Committee (BRAC) Strategy* (Kumarian Press, 1992).

Private Agencies Collaborating Together (PACT), *Asian Linkages: NGO Collaboration in the 1990s* (PACT, 1989).

Rothchild, Donald and Naomi Chazan (eds), *The Precarious Balance: State and Society in Africa* (Westview Press, 1988).

Sheth, D.L. and Harsh Sethi, 'The NGO Sector in India: Historical Context and Current Discourse', 2, *Voluntas*, 2, 49–68 (1991).

14 Human Rights and Developing Countries

Craig Webster and David Louis Cingranelli

The study of human rights in developing countries has academic, legal and policy dimensions. The primary academic challenge is to develop a human rights theory explaining differences in human rights policies and practices among governments. The central legal question is: how can national and international laws be used to protect human rights when the international system is an anarchy with no central law giver and enforcer? The main policy concern is what factors, manipulable through public policy, lead to human rights improvement. The authors of the publications included here address all three of these important human rights concerns but, because the focus of this volume is on policy analysis, we have selected publications that are especially useful for those interested in the systematic, scientific study of human rights. We have grouped the citations into four categories: data sources, measurement strategies, human rights and foreign policy, and explanations for variations in human rights practices among developing countries.

Human Rights Data Sources

Amnesty International Report (annual), London: Amnesty International Publications.
Country Reports on Human Rights Practices (annual), Washington, DC: US Government Printing Office.
Freedom House (annual), *Freedom in the World: Political Rights and Civil Liberties*, New York: Freedom Press.
Human Rights in Developing Countries Yearbook (annual), The Hague: Kluwer Law International.

Humana, Charles (1986), *World Human Rights Guide*, New York: Facts on File Publications.
UNICEF (United Nations Children's Fund) (1992), *The State of the World's Children 1992*, New York: Oxford University Press.
United Nations Development Programme (1991–), *Human Development Report*, New York: Oxford University Press.

Measurement of Human Rights

Bollen, Kenneth (1986), 'Political Rights and Political Liberties in Nations: an Evaluation of Human Rights Measures, 1950–1984', *Human Rights Quarterly*, **8**, (4), 567–591.
Cingranelli, David L. (ed.) (1988), *Human Rights: Theory and Measurement*, New York: St Martin's Press.
Cingranelli, David L. and Kevin Wright (1988), 'Correlates of Due Process' in David Louis Cingranelli (ed.), *Human Rights: Theory and Measurement*, London: Macmillan/Policy Studies Organization.
Donnelly, Jack and Rhoda E. Howard (1988), 'Assessing National Human Rights Performance: a Theoretical Framework', *Human Rights Quarterly*, **10**, (2), 214–48.
Gibney, Mark and Matthew Dalton (1996), 'The Political Terror Scale', in David Louis Cingranelli (ed.), *Human Rights and Developing Countries*, Greenwich, Connecticut: JAI Press, pp. 73–84.
Goldstein, Robert Justin (1986), 'The Limitations of Using Quantitative Data in Studying Human Rights Abuses', *Human Rights Quarterly*, **8**, (4), 607–27.
Haas, Michael (1996), 'Empirical Dimensions of Human Rights', in David Louis Cingranelli (ed.), *Human Rights and Developing Countries*, Greenwich, Connecticut: JAI Press, pp. 43–72.
Innes, Judith Eleanor (1992), 'Human Rights Reporting as a Policy Tool', in Thomas B. Jabine and Richard P. Claude (eds), *Human Rights and Statistics: Getting the Record Straight*, Philadelphia: University of Pennsylvania Press, pp. 235–57.
Jabine, Thomas B. and Richard P. Claude (eds) (1992), *Human Rights and Statistics: Getting the Record Straight*, Philadelphia: University of Pennsylvania Press.
McCamant, John F. (1981), 'A Critique of Present Measures of "Human Rights Development" and an Alternative', in Ved P. Nanda, James R. Scarritt and George W. Shepherd (eds), *Global Human Rights: Public Policies, Comparative Measures and NGO Strategies*, Boulder: Westview Press, pp. 123–46.

McNitt, Andrew D. (1988), 'Some Thoughts on the Systematic Measurement of the Abuse of Human Rights', in David Louis Cingranelli (ed.), *Human Rights: Theory and Measurement*, London: Macmillan/Policy Studies Organization, pp. 89–103.

Mitchell, Christopher, Michael Stohl, David Carleton and George A. Lopez (1986), 'State Terrorism: Issues of Concept and Measurement', in Michael Stohl and George A. Lopez (eds), *Government Violence and Repression: An Agenda for Research*, New York: Greenwood Press, pp. 1–26.

Stohl, Michael, David Carleton, George Lopez and Steven Samuels (1986), 'State Violation of Human Rights: Issues and Problems of Measurement', *Human Rights Quarterly*, 8, (4), 592–606.

Human Rights and Foreign Policy

Andreassen, Baard Anders (1982), 'Democratization and Human Rights Beyond Borders: On the Donor Recipient Connection', in Pearson Nherere and Marina D'Engelbronner-Kolff (eds), *Institutionalization of Human Rights in South Africa*, Oslo: Nordic Human Rights Publications.

Berry, Victoria and Allan McChesney (1988), 'Human Rights and Foreign Policy Making', in Robert O. Matthews and Cranford Pratt (eds), *Human Rights in Canadian Foreign Policy*, Kingston: McGill-Queen's University Press.

Cameron, Maxwell A. and Maureen Appel Molot (1995), *Canada Among Nations Democracy and Foreign Policy*, Ottawa: Carleton University Press.

Carleton, David and Michael Stohl (1985), 'The Foreign Policy of Human Rights: Rhetoric and Reality from Jimmy Carter to Ronald Reagan', *Human Rights Quarterly*, 7, (November), 202–29.

Carleton, David and Michael Stohl (1987), 'The Role of Human Rights in US Foreign Assistance Policy: A Critique and Reappraisal', *American Journal of Political Science*, 31, 1002–18.

Chomsky, Noam and Edward S. Herman (1979), *The Political Economy of Human Rights: The Washington Connection and Third World Fascism*, Boston: South End Press.

Cingranelli, David L. and Thomas E. Pasquarello (1985), 'Human Rights and the Distribution of US Foreign Aid to Latin American Countries', *American Journal of Political Science*, 29, 539–63.

Egeland, Jan (1988), *Impotent Superpower-Potent Small State*, Oslo: Norwegian University Press.

Forsythe, David P. (1988), *Human Rights and U.S. Foreign Policy: Congress Reconsidered*, Gainesville: University Press of Florida.

Forsythe, David P. (1989a), *Human Rights and World Politics*, rev. 2nd edn, Lincoln: University of Nebraska Press.

Forsythe, David P. (1989b), 'US Economic Assistance and Human Rights: Why the Emperor has (Almost) no Clothes', in David P. Forsythe (ed.), *Human Rights and Development: International Views*, New York: St Martin's Press.

Forsythe, David P. (1991), *The Internationalization of Human Rights*, Lexington: Lexington-Heath.

Fraser, Donald M. (1979), 'Human Rights and U.S. Foreign Policy', *International Studies Quarterly*, 23, (2), (June), 174–85.

Gang, Ira N. and James A. Lehman (1990), 'New Directions or Not: USAID in Latin America', *World Development*, 18, 5, (May), 723–32.

Hill, Dilys M. (ed.) (1989), *Human Rights and Foreign Policy: Principles and Practice*, London: Macmillan.

Kjekshus, Helge (1989), 'Development Aid and Human Rights: Some Observations by the Norwegian Ministry of Development Cooperation', in Lars Adam Rehof and Claus Gulmann (eds), *Human Rights in Domestic Law and Development Assistance Policies of the Nordic Countries*, Dordrecht, The Netherlands: Martinus Nijhoff Publishers.

Kommers, Donald P. and Gilburt D. Loescher (eds) (1979), *Human Rights and American Foreign Policy*, Notre Dame: University of Notre Dame Press.

Lebovic, James H. (1988), 'National Interests and US Foreign Aid: The Carter and Reagan Years', *Journal of Peace Research*, 25, (June), 115–35.

McCormick, James M. and Neil Mitchell (1988), 'Is U.S. Aid Really Linked to Human Rights in Latin America?', *American Journal of Political Science*, 32, 231–9.

McCormick, James M. and Neil Mitchell (1989), 'Human Rights and Foreign Assistance: An Upgrade', *Social Science Quarterly*, 70, 967–79.

McKinlay, R.D. and R. Little (1977), 'A Foreign Policy Model of U.S. Bilateral Aid Allocation', *World Politics*, 33, (October), 58–86.

McKinlay, R.D. and R. Little (1979), 'The U.S. Aid Relationship: A Test of Recipient Need and the Donor Interest Models', *Political Studies*, 27, (2), 236–50.

Mower, Glenn A. (1987), *Human Rights and American Foreign Policy: The Carter and Reagan Experiences*, New York: Greenwood Press.

Pasquarello, Thomas E. (1988), 'Human Rights and U.S. Bilateral Aid Allocations to Africa', in David L. Cingranelli (ed.), *Human Rights: Theory and Measurement*, New York: St Martin's Press.

Payaslian, Simon (1996), 'Human Rights and US Bilateral Assistance to Developing Countries: the Bush Administration, 1989–1990', in David

Cingranelli (ed.), *Human Rights and Developing Countries*, Greenwich, Connecticut: JAI Press, pp. 163–82.
Petersen, John H. (1976), 'Economic Interests and U.S. Foreign Policy in Latin America: An Empirical Approach', in Satish Raichur and Craig Liske (eds), *The Politics of Aid, Trade and Investment*, New York: Wiley-Halsted.
Poe, Steven C. (1991a), 'Human Rights and the Allocation of U.S. Military Assistance', *Journal of Peace Research*, 28, 205–16.
Poe, Steven C. (1991b), 'Human Rights and U.S. Foreign Aid: A Review of Quantitative Studies and Suggestions for Future Research', *Human Rights Quarterly*, 12, 499–512.
Poe, Steven C. (1992), 'Human Rights and Economic Aid Allocation Under Ronald Reagan and Jimmy Carter', *American Journal of Political Science*, 36 (1), 147–67.
Poe, Steven and Rangsima Sirirangsi (1993), 'Human Rights and U.S. Economic Aid to Africa', in *International Interactions* 18, pp. 309–22.
Pratt, Cornford (1994), *Canadian International Development Assistance Policies: An Appraisal*, Montreal and Kingston: McGill-Queen's University Press.
Rehof, Lars Adam (1989), 'Development Assistance from the Point of View of Human Rights', in Lars Adam Rehof and Claus Gulmann (eds), *Human Rights in Domestic Law and Development Assistance Policies of the Nordic Countries*, Dordrecht, The Netherlands: Martinus Nijhoff Publishers.
Schoultz, Lars (1981), *Human Rights and U.S. Policy Towards Latin America*, Princeton: Princeton University Press.
Sikkink, Kathryn (1991), 'The effectiveness of U.S. human rights policy: the case of Argentina and Guatemala', paper presented at the XVI International Congress of the Latin American Studies Association, Washington, DC.
Stohl, Michael, David Carleton and Steven E. Johnson (1984), 'Human Rights and U.S. Foreign Assistance from Nixon to Carter', *Journal of Peace Research*, 21, 215–26.
Stokke, Olav (ed.) (1985), 'Norwegian Development Cooperation Policy: Altruism and International Solidarity', in Johan Holst (ed.), *Norwegian Foreign Policy in the 1980s*, Oslo: Norwegian University Press.
Stokke, Olav (ed.) (1989), 'Determinants of Norwegian Aid Policy', in Olav Stokke (ed.), *Western Middle Powers and Global Poverty*, Uppsala: The Scandinavian Institute of African Studies.
Stokke, Olav (ed.) (1991), 'The Evaluation Policy and Performance of Norway', in Olav Stokke (ed.), *Evaluating Development Assistance: Policies and Performance*, London: Frank Cass.

Stokke, Olav (ed.) (1995), *Aid and Political Conditionality*, London: Frank Cass.
Vincent, R.J. (1986), *Human Rights and International Relations*, Cambridge: Cambridge University Press.
Webster, Craig (1996), 'US Foreign Policy and Human Rights in Latin America: An Empirical Investigations Over Three Presidencies', in David Cingranelli (ed.), *Human Rights and Developing Countries*, Greenwich, Connecticut: JAI Press, pp. 183–92.

Explanations for Human Rights Practices

Arat, Z. (1991), *Democracy and Human Rights in Developing Countries*, Boulder: Lynne Rienner.
Avery, William P. and David P. Rapkin (1989), *Markets, Politics and Change in the Global Political Economy*, Boulder: Lynne Rienner..
Bornschier, Volker and Christopher Chase-Dunn (1985), *Transnational Corporations and Underdevelopment*, New York: Praeger.
Carleton, David (1989), 'The New International Division of Labor, Export-oriented Growth and State Repression in Latin America', in George A. Lopez and Michael Stohl (eds), *Dependence, Development and State Repression*, New York: Greenwood Press, pp. 211–36.
Claude, Richard P. (ed.) (1976), *Comparative Human Rights*, Baltimore: Johns Hopkins University Press.
Forsythe, David (1991), *The Internationalization of Human Rights*, Lexington: Lexington–Heath.
Gurr, Ted Robert (1986), 'The Political Origins of State Violence and Terror: A Theoretical Analysis', in Michael Stohl and George A. Lopez (eds), *Government Violence and Repression*, New York: Greenwood Press, pp. 45–71.
Henderson, Conway, W. (1991), 'Conditions Affecting the Use of Political Repression', *Journal of Conflict Resolution*, **35**, (1), 120–42.
Henderson, Conway W. (1996), 'Dependency and Political Repression: A Caveat on Research Expectations', in David Louis Cingranelli (ed.), *Human Rights and Developing Countries*, Greenwich, Connecticut: JAI Press, pp. 101–14.
Hirsch, Leonard Paul (1986), 'Incorporation Into the World Economy: Empirical Tests of Dependency Theory', in Mary Ann Tetreault and Charles Frederick Abel (eds), *Dependency Theory and the Return of High Politics*, New York: Greenwood Press, pp. 101–21.
Jackson, Steven, Bruce Russett, Duncan Snidal and David Sylvan (1978),

'Conflict and Coercion in Dependent States', *Journal of Conflict Resolution*, **22**, (4), 627–57.
Klare, Michael T. and Cynthia Arnson (1981), *Supplying Repression*, Washington, DC: Institute for Policy Studies.
Kowalewski, David (1989), 'Asian State Repression and Strikes Against Transnationals', in George A. Lopez and Michael Stohl (eds), *Dependence, Development and State Repression*, New York: Greenwood Press, pp. 67–93.
Lopez, George A. (1986), 'National Security Ideology as an Impetus to State Violence and State Terror', in Michael Stohl and George A. Lopez (eds), *Government Violence and Repression*, New York: Greenwood Press, pp. 73–95.
Lopez, George A. and Michael Stohl (1989a), 'Introduction: The Development Dependence Factors of State Repression', in George A. Lopez and Michael Stohl (eds), *Dependence, Development and State Repression*, New York: Greenwood Press, pp. ix–xv.
Lopez, George A. and Michael Stohl (eds) (1989b), *Dependence, Development and State Repression*, New York: Greenwood Press.
Mitchell, Neil J. and James N. McCormick (1988), 'Economic and Political Explanations of Human Rights Violations', *World Politics*, **40**, (4), 476–98.
Muller, Edward N. (1985), 'Dependent Economic Development, Aid Dependence on the United States, and Democratic Breakdown in the Third World', *International Studies Quarterly*, **29** (4), 445–69.
Poe, Steve and C. Neal Tate (1994), 'Repression of Personal Integrity in the 1980s: A Global Analysis', *American Political Science Review*, **88** (December), 853–72.
Pritchard, Kathleen J. (1989), 'Human Rights and Development: Theory and Data', in David P. Forsythe (ed.), *Human Rights and Development: International Views*, New York: St Martin's Press.
Rothgeb, Jr., John M. (1989), 'Direct Foreign Investment, Repression, Reform and Political Conflict in Third World States', in William P. Avery and David P. Rapkin (eds), *Markets, Politics, and Change in the Global Political Economy*, Boulder: Lynne Rienner, pp. 105–25.
Schwartz, C. Michael and Harry R. Targ (1989), 'Agricultural Development, Political Violence and State Militarization in Central America', in George A. Lopez and Michael Stohl (eds), *Dependence, Development and State Repression*, New York: Greenwood Press, pp. 237–56.
Scoble, Harry M. and Laurie S. Wiseberg (1981), 'Problems of Comparative Research on Human Rights', in Ved P. Nanda, James R. Scarritt and George W. Shepherd (eds), *Global Human Rights: Public Policies, Com-*

parative Measures and NGO Strategies, Boulder: Westview Press, pp. 147–72.

Spalding, N. (1988), 'Democracy and Economic Human Rights in the Third World', in D. Cingranelli (ed.), *Human Rights: Theory and Measurement*, London: Macmillan, pp. 173–89.

Spalding, N. (1990), 'The relevance of basic needs for political and economic development', *Studies in Comparative International Development*, **25**, (3), 90–115.

Tetreault, Mary Ann and Charles Frederick Abel (1986), *Dependency Theory and the Return of High Politics*, New York: Greenwood Press.

Wolpin, Miles (1986), 'State Terrorism and Repression in the Third World: Parameters and Prospects', in Michael Stohl and George A. Lopez (eds), *Government Violence and Repression*, New York: Greenwood Press, pp. 97–164.

Ziegenhagen, Eduard A. (1996), 'Patterns of Due Process Protections of Human Rights within and Among Nations', in David Louis Cingranelli (ed.), *Human Rights and Developing Countries*, Greenwich, Connecticut: JAI Press, pp. 115–30.

Index

Ability to pay, 14
Abkhazia, 30
Abortions, 32
Accountability, 9
Administrative Staff College,
 Hyderabad, 126
Adult education, 62
Afghanistan, 18, 53
Africa, 29, 43, 133
 suggestions from, 3
 workshops, 141
Age groups, conflicts between, 7
Agency for International Development, 31
Agriculture, 30, 31, 32
Alternative dispute resolution, 46
Alternative public policies, xv
Alternative world order, 46
American
 bases in Philippines, 49
 foreign aid, 60
 military bases, 8
Analysis, policy, xv
Angola, 18
Angola-Mozambique, 29
Anti-discrimination, 30
 legislation, 36
Armenia, 18, 30
Arms control and international security, 46
Asia, 29, 43, 133
 workshops, 141
Azerbaijan, 18, 30

Bad exporting, 85
Bangkok, Thailand workshop, 38
Bangladesh, 17
Beijing University, 38
Beijing, China, 38
Bibliographies, Developmental Policy
 Studies: The Relevant Literature, 151
Bibliographies, xvi
Bibliography on developmental policy
 studies, xvi
Bibliography on human rights, xvi
Bill or Rights, 83
Biological science, 34
Birth control, information and devices
 for, 32
Bolivia, 30
Bombay, 38
Bosnia
 and Herzegovina, 18
 postwar developments, 29
 recognition as sovereign state, 35
Branches and levels of government, xv, 30
Brazil, 30
Burundi, 18
Business administration, 11
Business consumers, 30

Cambodia, 18
Camp David Accords, 47
Capitalism vs socialism, 90
Caucusus, 29
Ceasefires, 26

Central America, 30
Central governments and secessionist provinces, disputes between, 49, 63
Central Policy Review Staff, 121
Chechnya, 30
China, 29, 85, 87
  and Thailand, 80
  supplementary ideas from, 6
Chinese public administration, 9
Chulalongkorn University, 38, 80
CIA (Central Intelligence Agency), 17, 27
Citizen participation in socioeconomic development, 46
Civil liberties, 36
Civil rights, 44
Civilian government vs military government, 77
Clark Air Base, 58
Classes, conflicts between, 7
College of Public Administration in the Philippines, 121, 126
Columbia, 30
Communication, 31, 32
Commuting to and from Manila, 8
Comparative government, 111
Competition, as stimulus, 6
Composition and size of the training group, 124
Conflict resolution, 44, 46
Conflicting economic classes with international implications, disputes between, 72
Conflicting nations within a country, disputes between, 67
Conflicts
  between age groups, 7
  between classes, 7
  between ethnic groups, 7
  between the education levels, 7
  between the sexes, 7
  between the social divisions, 7
Conservative
  alternative of nuclear arms/Star Wars, 50
  or elitist goal, 12, 13
  or nationalistic goal of avoiding being conquered/conquering the other side, 50
Consortium on Peace Research, Education and Development, 48
Consumption and domestic, 15
Contents of short-term training courses, 129
Contents of the course, 125
Contraceptives, 32
Controlling countries and their colonies or quasi-colonies, disputes between, 49, 56
Cooperative farming, use of, 4
Copyright, international piracy, 107
Corn-growing techniques, use of, 3
Counsel, right to, 36
Course duration and contents, 125
Course, structure, 123
Courts, 35
Credit
  for seeds, pesticides, herbicides and farm equipment in land reform programs, 62
  rather than cash, 62
  specifically earmarked, 62
Crime reduction, 30, 35
Criminal justice system, 30, 35
Croatia, 20
  secession from Yugoslavia, 64
Cross-examine, right to, 36
Cuba, 17
Customers, xvi

Decision analysis, 11
Defense and investment, 15
Deficit, dealing with the, 15
Democracy, xvi, 30, 93
  vs dictatorship, 90
  world moving toward, 81
Democratic rights, 83
Department of Transportation, 31
Developing nations, xv, xvi
Developmental Policy Studies Consortium, 27

Developmental Policy Studies: The Relevant Literature, 151
Developmental policy, bibliography on, xvi
Dialogues and dialectics: New synthesis in a civil society, 156
Dictatorship vs democracy, 90
Disputes between
   central governments and secessionist provinces, 49
   controlling countries and their colonies or quasi-colonies, 49
   economic class conflict with international implications, 49
   national or ethnic groups within a country, 49
   pro-democracy uprisings, 49
   sovereign nations, 49
   Soviet Nations, 50
Disputes:
   central governments and secessionist provinces, xvi
   conflicting classes with international implications, xvi
   conflicting nations within a country, xvi
Districting, 34
Dollar Exchange Rates, 108
Domestic and consumption, 15
Due process, xvi, 36, 85
Duration of the course, 125

Eastern Europe, 29
Ecology, 44
Economic
   class conflict with international implications, disputes between, 49
   communities, international, 108
   development and well being, 46
   policy, 30, 31, 37, 43
Economy, 29
Education, 43
   and training in public policy, 119
   levels, conflicts between 7
Educational development, put resources into, 6

Effectiveness, 10, 11
Egypt, 29
El Salvador, 30
Electrification, more, 4
Emergencies of natural disasters worsened by bad societal planning, 17
Emergency nations, xvi, 17
Emigrants, 101
Employment, 43
Energy, 30, 31, 32, 34
   and electricity production, improve, 62
Engineering, 11, 30
   and science policy, 33
Equal treatment, 5, 35, 36, 85
Equity, 10, 11
Eritrea, 20
Ethiopia, 20
Ethnic groups, conflicts between, 7
Europe workshops, 141
Europe, 133
European Community, 31
European/non-European contributions, 43, 44
Evaluating alternative positions on tariffs, 96
Exchange of
   factories, 102
   free speech ideas, 105
   goods, 93
   people, 99
Explanations for human rights practices, 163
Exporting Democratic rights, 81
Exporting other US products, 85

Factories, exchange of, 102
Factories, US going abroad, 104
Fair Labor Standards Act (FLSA), 104
Fair procedure in criminal proceedings, 5
Family planning, 32
Farm equipment, sharing of, 4
Farm products, negotiating free trade in, 97

Federal Communications Commission, 31
Financial administration, 13
Financial resources, lack of, xvi
Financing, 9
FLSA (Fair Labor Standards Act), 104
Food and water standards, 17
Food stamps system, 32
Food, 43
Foreign Factories in the United States, 102
Foreign policy, and human rights, 161
Format, implementation and feedback, 134
Free enterprise, 87
Free flow of ideas, xvi
Free flow of people, xvi
Free marketplace of ideas, 6
Free speech, xvi, 84, 85, 87, 105
Freedom of
  assembly, 6
  speech, 5, 30, 35, 36
  press, 6

Guatemala, 30
General exchange facilitators, 108
General peace and conflict studies, 46
Georgia, 20, 30
Georgia, 30
Getting Japan and other countries to reduce tariffs, 96
Glasnost, 87
Global education, 43
Global policy studies, 111, 112
Good exporting, 86
Goods, 111
Government Organizational Manual, 31
Government
  branches and levels of, xv
  policy, xvi
  repression, 26
  structures, xv
Governmental incentives, increasing national income through, 5
Greece, 85
Growth, economic, 31

Guide to Careers and Graduate Education in Peace Studies, 46

Haiti, 20, 30
Health and technological innovation, 30, 34
Health care and housing, improve, 62
Health maintenance organization, 34
Health, education, and welfare problems, 111
High goals, setting, 6
Hong Kong, 16
Housing, 30
  need to be privatized, 33
How fields differ from related fields, 111
Human rights
  and developing countries, 159
  and ecological balance, 46
  and foreign policy, 161
  bibliography on, xvi
  data sources, 159
  encourage, 5
  measurement of, 160
  practices, explanations for, 164
Humanitarians, 88

IASIA (International Association of Schools and Institutes of Administration), 119
Ideology vs technology, 10
IDR (International Dispute Resolution), 37
IDR workshop, 80
IEC (International Economic Communities), 114
Improved medical technology, 30
Improving
  aid to developing countries, 3
  developmental policy, 3
  International Competitiveness, 93
Income tax, 14
Increased productivity, 30
Increasing national income, 5
India, 29
Industrialized nations, xv

Inexpensive energy, 30
Inflation, 30, 31
Institut International d'Administration Publique, 126
Intense conflicts, 26
International Association of Schools and Institutes of Administration (IASIA), 119
International
  competitiveness, improving, 93
  Copyright Piracy, 107
  dispute resolution (IDR), xvi, 37, 49
  dispute resolution workshop, 79
  Economic Communities (IEC), 108, 114
  economic communities and super-optimum solutions, 69
  interaction, participate in more, 7, 11
  Organization and law, 46
  Peace Academy, 47
  peace, 93
  prosperity, xvi, 93
  Refugees, 101
  relations, 30, 35, 111
  trade, 30
Inventors, no monopolistic patents, 34
Investment and defense, 15
Investment outlets, xvi
Iraq, 20, 29
Iraq's invasion of Kuwait, 45
Israel

Japan, 16, 55
Japan, getting her to reduce tariffs, 96
Joint perspective, 50
Jordon, 29
Judge, right to have a, 36
Judicial review, 34

Kennedy-Johnson Vietnam War, 90
Korean War, 45
Kuwait, 29

Labor, 30
Land reform in Pakistan, 50
Land reform programs credit for, 62

Land use, 30
Latin America Workshops, 141
Latin America, 30, 43, 133
League of Nations, 90
Lebanon, 29
Legal issues, 35
Legal policy, 30, 32
Legal policy, 35, 37
Legal system, 29
Lenin, 10
Levels and branches of government, xv
Liberal alternative of unilateral disarmament, 50
Liberal or democratic goal, 12, 13
Liberal or pacifist goal of avoiding nuclear war, 50
Liberia, 22, 29
Libya, 29
Literacy, programs to raise, 4
Literature used, 128

Management science, 11
Man-made crises, 17
Manufacturing, 31
Mao, 10
Marshall Plan, 86
Marx, 10
Mass labor, use of, 3
Measurement of human rights, 160
Medical care, 43
Medical care, low-cost, high leverage, 4
Merit treatment, xvi, 30
Methods of teaching, 127
Mexico, 30
Middle East, 29
Military government vs civilian government, 77
Minimum wage problem, 8
Minority viewpoints, 30
Moldova, 29
Monroe Doctrine, 87
More than one political party, 6
Mozambique, 22
Multiple dimensions, 112
Multiple interest groups, 6

172 Policy Within and Across Developing Nations

Mutually beneficial interactions, with PSO, 7

NAFTA (North American Free Trade Agreement), 68, 98
Napoleonic code, 35
National Interest criteria, 88
National or ethnic groups within a country, disputes between, 49
National sovereignty, 59
Nations, developing, xv
Nations, industrialized, xv
Natural disasters, 17
Negotiating free trade in farm products, 97
Neutral alternative of conventional arms development, 50
Neutral goal of being politically feasible, 50
Neutral goal of reducing the burden on the economy, 50
New Delhi, 38
New synthesis in a civil society, dialogues and dialectics, 156
Nicaragua, 30, 53
Nigeria, 17
Nixon's anti-communism, 90
Non-European/European contributions, 43, 44
North America, 133
North American Free Trade Agreement (NAFTA), 98
North Korea, 22
Nuclear Arms in South Asia, 140

Oceans, Antarctica, or the atmosphere, problems of, 111
Office of Technology Assessment, 31
On-the-Job Training (OJT), 11, 31, 62
Operations research, 11
Ossetia, 30

Pakistan, 29
Palestinian Authority, 29
Panama, 30
Party systems, 30

Past US Foreign Policy, 137, 138
Peace and justice in the religious context, 46
Peace and World Order Studies: A Curriculum Guide, 46
Peace chronicle and Peace and Change, 48
Peace Corps, 63, 101
Peace Research Abstracts Journal, 48
Peace Research Centers, 47
Peace Research Institute, 47
Peace Studies and Research Centers, 43
Peace Studies Programs, 46
Peace, xvi
People, 111
People's Republic of China, 10, 16
People's University, 38
Perception of reality, 44
Perestroika, 87
Personnel, 9
  administration, 11
  management, 10
  recruitment, 12
Perspectives on their source and impact, political institutions as the missing component in adjustment programs, 154
Peru, 30
Philippine
  economy, credits for buying American products and services, 62
  elementary and secondary education, upgrading, 62
  energy and electricity production, improve, 62
  health care and housing, improve, 62
  health care and housing, relevant credits, 62
  higher education, upgrading, 62
  land reform and super-optimizing analysis, 72
  land reform programs, 62
  productivity, improve, 62
  suburban job opportunities, subsidize, 62
Philippines, 7, 85

Index 173

Philippines, American bases in, 50, 57
Physical planning, 33
Physics, 11
Pluralistic society, encourage, 6
Policies public, xv
Policy across developing nations, xv
Policy analysis, xv
 training for developmental administrators, 119
 training program, proposed, 143
Policy reform and its impacts, restructuring distressed economics, 153
Policy Studies Organization, 7
Policy within developing nations, xv
Political institutions as the missing component in adjustment programs: perspectives on their source and impact, 154
Political leaders, choosing, xv
Political policy, 30, 34, 37, 44
Political science and law professors, win friends and influence with, 5
Political science, 5, 111
Political settlements, 26
Political system, 29
Pollution, 30, 111
Population control, 30, 32
Positive incentive, use of, 7
Post-crises mop-up, 26
Poverty, 30
Pragmatic experimentation, need for, 6
Predictive or explanatory analysis, 112
Prescriptive or evaluative analysis, 112
Presidential form of government, 34
Problems of the oceans, Antarctica, or the atmosphere, 111
Pro-democracy movement in Thailand, 75
Pro-democracy movements, xvi
Pro-democracy uprisings, 49
Professional training, need for, 7
Promoting full employment and increased international competitiveness of US, 53, 54
Promoting the gross national product of the USA, 53, 54

Promoting the national security of the United States, 53, 54
Proposed policy analysis training program, 143
Prosperity, xvi, 30, 93
Pro-US arguments, 83
PSO World Regions, 141
Public administration, 5
Public funding of campaigns, 34
Public interest law, 46
Public law, 5
Public policies, xv
Public policy, 5
 in Bosnia, 37
 studies, 111
 16-points, 3

Raw materials, use of local, 3
Reagan Evil empire, 90
Reagan-Gorbachev agreements, 50
Reform, 8
Relevant Literature, Developmental Policy Studies, 151
Restructuring distressed economics: policy reform and its impacts, 153
Rewarding performance, 13
Royalties, inventors' exclusive rights to, 34
Rural to urban areas, move from, 4
Russia (Chechnya), 22, 55
Russian Academiy of Sciences, 38
Rwanda, 22
Rwanda-Burundi, 29

Sales tax, 14
Satellite dishes, collectively use of, 4
Schools system, 32
Schools, 30
Science policy, 30, 34
Seceding in South Asia, 140
Secession of Chechnya from RSFSR, 64
Secession of Croatia from Yugoslavia, 64
Semi-autonomous federalism, 34
Semi-sovereign federalism, 34

Serbia, 29
Sexes, conflicts between, 7
Shelter, 43
Short-term course in public policy, 122
Short-term courses, staffing, 128
Short-term training courses, contents, 129
Short-term training program, 120
Sierra Leone, 22
Simmering conflicts, 26
Single-member districts, 34
Single-payer system health care, 34
Size and composition of the training group, 124
Smoot-Hawley Tariff, 90
Social divisions, conflicts between, 7
Social policy, 30, 32, 37
Socialism vs Capitalism, 90
Society, 29
Somalia, 24, 29
SOS alternative of bilateral arms reduction, 50
South Africa, 85
South China, 16
South Korea, 16
Sovereign nations, disputes between, 49
Soviet Nations, disputes between, 50
Soviet Union, 55
Soybeans as protein, 3
Soybeans, use of, 3
Sri Lanka, 17, 24
Staffing short-term courses, 128
Standards of food and water, 17
Stimulating investment, 14
Structure of the course, 123
Subic Naval Base, 58
Subsidies, well-placed, 85
Suburban job opportunities, credits for subsidizing, 62
Sudan, 24
Super-optimizing applied to
 civil war in Yugoslavia, 67
 land reform in the Philippines, 72
 Russian secession, 63
Super-optimizing perspective on US-USSR negotiations, 50
Super-optimum solution, 8, 12, 60
 and international economic communities, 69
Suppliers, xvi
Synthetic agricultural products, more use of, 4
Syria, 29
Systematic policy analysis, need for, 4, 6

Taiwan, 16
Tajikistan, 24, 29
Tariffs, xvi
 evaluating alternative positions on, 96
 getting Japan and other countries to reduce, 96
Tax benefits and subsidies for foreign factories, 102
Tax breaks, 85
Tax sources, 14
Taxes, 15
Technological innovation, 34
Technologically innovative products, 85
Technology transfer, xvi
Technology, 29, 37
Thailand, 16
 and China, 80
 civilian vs military government, 77
 crisis case study, implications from, 77
 democracy, 50
 crisis case study, implications from, 77
 IDR workshop, 80
 pro-democracy movement and uprising, 75
Third World cultures, 43
Tiananmen Square, China, 50
Topical Workshops, 142
Trade and Human Rights, 105
Training administrations and policy makers, xvi
Training group, size and composition, 124

Training program, 32
Training the young, 30
Training, for developmental administrators, 119
Training, policy analysis, 119
Trans-boundary problems, 111
Transport, 31
Trilingualism in Philippine education, 8
Truman Doctrine, 90
Turkey, 85
Two-party system, 34

Unemployment, 30, 31
United States Institute of Peace, 43, 47
United States military bases in the Philippines, 57
United States, 31, 55
United States, should encourage use of pluralistic/pragmatic systems, 7
University of Philippines, 38
Upgrading Philippine elementary and secondary education, 62
Upgrading Philippine higher education, 62
Uprising in Thailand, 75
US factories going abroad, 104
US immigration policy, 99

USIA win-win traveling seminars, 133
USSR-US problem, 49

Vietnam War, 45, 85
Volunteerism in Technical Assistance, 101
Voter turnout, encouraging high, 34

War, 44
Water and food standards, 17
West Germany, 16, 55
Western Sahara, 29
Win-win
  analysis workshops, 27
  developmental administration, 9
  issues in South Asia, 138
  or super-optimizing perspectives, 9
  policy analysis, xvi
  solutions rather than tradeoffs, 6
  US Foreign Policy, 135, 136
  workshops, 37
World Bank, 31, 126
World moving toward democracy, 81
World peace, 30
World War I, 45
World-wide democracy, xvi
Wrongdoing, notice of, 36